OTHER NITTY GRITTY COOKBOOKS

The Compleat American Housewife 1776
LOW CARBOHYDRATE COOKBOOK
THE WORLD IN ONE MEAL
KID'S COOKBOOK
ITALIAN
FIRST BRANDY COOKBOOK
CHEESE GUIDE & COOKBOOK
MILLER'S GERMAN
QUICHE & SOUFFLE
TO MY DAUGHTER, WITH LOVE
NATURAL FOODS
CHINESE VEGETARIAN
FOUR SEASONS PARTY BOOK
WORKING COUPLES
MEXICAN
PARIS....and then some
SUNDAY BREAKFAST
FISHERMAN'S WHARF
CHARCOAL
ICE CREAM COOKBOOK
HIPPO HAMBURGER
GOURMET BLENDER
THE WOK, a Chinese Cookbook
CHRISTMAS COOKBOOK
CAST IRON
JAPANESE COUNTRY
FONDUE

DEDICATION:

To my grandmothers, both of whom were superb cooks.

In the face of grinding poverty, they prepared food with lots of love and lots of spices, creating delicious delicacies with limited supplies, thereby earning the title of 'balaboosta' – the highest accolade accorded a Jewish cook.

Through my father's memories, I was able to re-create the dishes his mother had served, and through my mother's recollections I recaptured her mother's favorites. From this legacy and from trips to Israel and the Middle East with my husband, I have compiled this book of favorite Jewish recipes.

THE MARKET'S FULL OF TRADERS
AS IT WAS HUNDREDS OF YEARS AGO

The Jewish Gourmet Cookbook

by Pauline Frankel

Illustrations by Mike Nelson

A Nitty Gritty Book*
Published by
Nitty Gritty Productions
P.O. Box 5457
Concord, California 94524

ISBN: 0-911954-18-X

FOREWORD

There is something special about Jewish cooking for Jewish people. The extremely high quality of the kosher ingredients combined with the deliciously unique flavors inherent in this hearty, wholesome food, is so delightfully unlike the fancy sauces of French and Italian fare, that the Jewish diner feels at home.

The purpose of this book is to bring together a selection of better-known Jewish recipes into one easily handled book, so that Jews can easily prepare their favorite familiar foods, and gentiles can learn what it's all about.

The world of kosher dining is not normally considered to be one that attracts the gourmet. Yet no one should consider himself a gourmet who has not become thoroughly familiar with this modern, wholesome cuisine. So, set your table with your fanciest china and best silver, and delight your family and friends with these traditional Jewish recipes from the JEWISH GOURMET COOKBOOK.

FACES OF ISRAEL

CONTENTS

GLOSSARY OF JEWISH WORDS AND PHRASES

Part of the fun of Jewish cooking is getting to know the unique Hebrew words and phrases that not only will help you understand this book, but they will also let you know what your Jewish friends are talking about.

Balaboosta – an excellent homemaker
Bar Mitzvah – the acceptance ceremony of a 13-year-old boy.
Bubele – an endearing term used for loved ones
Chutzpah – gall, incredible nerve, effrontery
Eppes – a little
Essig – vinegar
Fleisch – meat
Gedempte – braised or steamed
Gelt – money
Haimische – warm, cozy, homelike
Kibbutznick – a member of a kibbutz in Israel

Kvell – to gush or dote over the achievements of a relative
Kvetching – complaining, griping, whining
Landsman – someone who comes from the same hometown (usually in Europe)
Mavin – an expert, a connoisseur
Mechaieh – a real joy or pleasure
Mishpocheh – family or clan in the larger sense
Pareve – foods that can be eaten with milk or meat, such as fish and vegetables
Sephardit – the Hebrew dialect spoken in the Middle East, Israel, and North Africa
Shabbat – the Hebrew Sabbath, from Friday sunset to Saturday sunset
Shevuot – the festival commemorating the Torah and the Ten Commandments
Tam – a very special flavor
Tzibbele – onions
Yenta – a gossipy woman, unable to keep a secret
Zoftig – juicy or fleshy (in our home this connoted overweight)

AMEL MARKET
N BEERSHEBA

Appetizers

The traditional Jewish menu always includes an appetizer. The most popular are gefilte fish, chopped liver, and herring, either plain or chopped. Appetizers such as matbeylah, humus, and felafel which are just as authentic, are better known in Israel and other parts of the Middle East. These appetizers double as either salads or spreads.

Knishes are well known on the wedding and Bar Mitzvah circuit. These tiny, piping hot hors d'oeuvres are perfect with cocktails or soup. Enjoy introducing yourself to these Jewish specialities.

CHOPPED LIVER

1 pound chicken livers
3 medium chopped onions
1/4 cup rendered chicken fat
2 hard-cooked egg yolks
1 teaspoon salt
Freshly ground black pepper
A pinch of sugar

Wash the livers and dry them on paper towels. Saute the onions in the fat until brown. Then push them to one side of the skillet and add the livers. Toss them until they have lost their red color. Turn the heat down to medium and simmer the livers for 10 minutes. Remove from the heat. Place all the ingredients in a food grinder using a fine blade. Season with the salt, pepper, and sugar. Taste and adjust the seasoning, if necessary. Serve in small scoops on lettuce leaves as a first course or as a spread for crackers or matzos. Serves 6 people as a first course or at least 12 as a spread.

PAREVE CHOPPED LIVER

1/4 cup oil
1 pound sliced mushrooms
1 hard-boiled egg
Salt and pepper to taste
1 medium chopped onion

Saute the onions until limp, add the mushrooms and cook until they are tender and the onions brown. Place all the ingredients in the blender, using a medium speed, until the mixture is smooth. Remove to a bowl and season to taste with salt and pepper. Can be made a day ahead and stored in the refrigerator. Serve at room temperature. Delicious on crackers or matzos or served in scoops on a bed of lettuce. Serves 4 as a first course or makes 2 cups of spread.

BAKED GEFILTE FISH: When you want to stop kvetching!

2 pounds EACH: whitefish, yellow pike, winter carp, skinned and filleted
1 large onion
2 teaspoons salt
Pepper to taste
3 large eggs
3/4 cup ice water (IMPORTANT)
Pinch of sugar
3 tablespoons matzo meal

Grind the fish with the onion twice using the fine blade of the food grinder. Remove to a large mixing bowl. Add the remaining ingredients. Adjust the seasoning to your taste. Turn the mixture into a 9x5x3-inch loaf pan; cover lightly with foil. Bake for 1 hour in a preheated 350° oven. Delicious served warm or cold. It should always be served with white and red horseradish. Accompany with sliced hard-boiled egg. Makes 6 to 8 generous servings.

CHOPPED HERRING

1 large jar pickled herring
1 small onion
2 hard-boiled eggs
1 green apple
2 slices firm-texture white bread
1/4 cup cider vinegar
Sugar to taste
Freshly ground black pepper

Place the herring, onion, eggs, and apple in a food grinder using a fine blade. Soak the bread in the vinegar; squeeze dry. Add it to the herring. Season to taste with sugar and pepper. Serve as a salad on lettuce or as a spread with rye breads, challah, and matzo.

FELAFEL

Felafel is the Israeli hot dog. There it is eaten from sidewalk stands in the same abundance that hot dogs are consumed in the United States.

Buy felafel mix in the import section of the market. It is a dry mix of chick-pea and flour with oriental spices. Follow the directions on the package, and shape the mixture into small balls. Use a deep-fat fryer set at 375° with 3 inches of fat in it. Fry for 2 to 3 minutes until crisp and golden on all sides. Drain and serve immediately on a hot platter. Pita (Arabic Bread), salad, and pickles are served with felafel. The salad consists of finely chopped lettuce and tomatoes, lightly dressed with lemon juice and olive oil, and seasoned with salt and pepper. The Druze restaurant on Mount Carmel near Haifa inserted a mild pickled chili pepper into the pita. It is invariably eaten as take-out food.

MATBEYLAH

1 medium eggplant
1/4 cup finely chopped onion
2 tablespoons olive oil
1/4 cup lemon juice
Salt to taste
Freshly ground pepper to taste
Sugar
Parsley

Bake the eggplant in a preheated 350° oven until tender, about 1 hour. Cool slightly; peel the eggplant. Mash it, leaving a lumpy texture. Add the remaining ingredients except parsley. Adjust the seasonings to your taste. Garnish with parsley sprigs. Serve with pita (Arabic Bread), rye bread, or crackers. This is eaten as a dip, using the pita or crackers as a pusher. You can mound it on a serving plate or arrange it like humus, looking like a tower with a moat around it.

HUMUS

1 can (1-pound) drained garbanzo beans
Juice of 2 lemons
2 cloves garlic
1/4 cup olive oil
1/2 thin slice onion

Salt and pepper to taste

Place all the ingredients except the seasonings in the blender. Blend until smooth. Turn the humus into a bowl; season to taste with salt and pepper. Serve the humus in a fairly flat plate. Swirl it a little with a spoon; drizzle a small amount of olive oil on it. Garnish with parsley sprigs. Serve at room temperature.

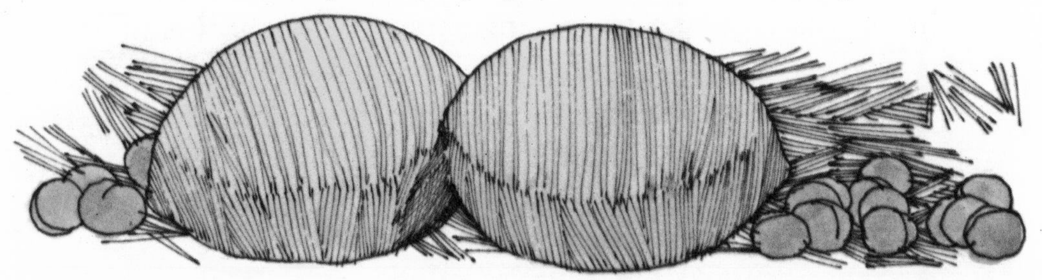

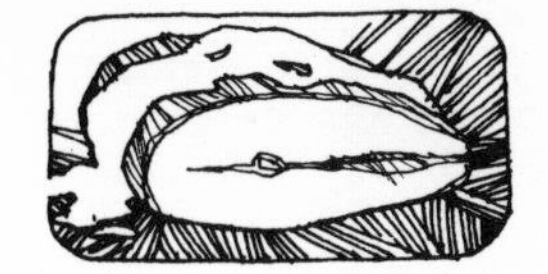

KNISHES

Dough: 1 package dry yeast
1/4 cup warm water
2 cups flour
1 tablespoon sugar
pinch salt
2 sticks margarine
3 large eggs
2 egg yolks + 1 teaspoon white, beaten lightly (for glaze)

Dissolve the yeast in warm water. Mix the flour, sugar, and salt in a large bowl. Cut the margarine into the dry ingredients until the pieces are tiny. Add the yeast and the egg yolks. Knead the mixture with your hands until it is smooth and holds together. Wrap the dough in waxed paper. Store in the refrigerator overnight.

Divide the dough into 4 equal parts; refrigerate them. Use a well-floured pastry cloth and rolling pin cover. Place 1/4 of the dough on the pastry cloth. Roll out into a large rectangle. The dough should be tissue paper thin. It can be patched if it tears. Place the filling in a 1-inch strip along the edge closest to you. Do not get any filling on the cloth. Roll like a jelly roll, resting the roll seam-side down. Cut into 1-inch slices; place on an ungreased cooky sheet. Cover with a linen towel. Let them rest until all the dough is used. Glaze the knishes with a mixture of the egg yolks and white. This makes them a rich golden brown. Bake in a preheated 400° oven for 20 minutes or until well browned. Remove from the cooky sheet; cool. When freezing them, separate the layers with foil.

To serve: Heat on a cooky sheet in a 400° oven for 18 to 20 minutes. They should be tongue-burning hot. After the first 5 to 8 minutes, lay a piece of foil over them. This makes 5 to 7 dozen.

Fillings:

Chopped Liver - Use the recipe on page 52.

Potato -

2 large chopped onions
1/4 cup chicken fat
2 cups hot mashed potatoes
1 large egg
Salt and freshly ground pepper to taste

Saute onions until brown; mix ingredients well; chill before use.

ACRE-MARKET

Soups

Making your own homemade soups is easy and very rewarding. I like to start making soup in the morning, when I can let it simmer gently on the stove as I work around the house or chat with the neighbors.

When making soup, it is essential that you not be in a hurry. Relax and let the blendings of the spices in the soup attain the fulfillment that only long, slow simmering can bring, and you will have a much richer-flavored soup. It is best to make the soup in advance, let it cool and 'ripen' for a few hours before serving, then bring it just to a high heat – do not boil – before serving.

Jewish soups are thick and hearty – whole meals, actually. Serve them with the meat in the soup bowl as is done in Israel, accompanied by breads and a salad, or serve the meat from the soup as the main course following the soup. Hot or cold, soup is a heart-warming way to begin a meal.

CHICKEN SOUP

Be sure to make this the day before you want to serve it, as chilling this soup overnight improves the flavor.

6 pounds chicken backs and necks
Several chicken feet
3 1/4 quarts water
3 peeled onions
2 cloves garlic
1 1/4 tablespoons salt
3 peeled carrots
A bunch parsley
Parsley root
Fresh or dried dill to taste

Prepare chicken feet by chopping off the nails, immersing the feet in boiling water for several minutes, and peeling the skin from them. Soak the chicken parts in cold water changing it frequently. Place the backs, necks, feet, water, and onions in a 12-quart pot. Bring to a boil, lower the heat, and simmer for 2 to 3 hours. Add the remaining ingredients; cover and simmer for another hour or more. Strain the soup; place it in a clean pot, and refrigerate overnight.

Chicken Soup Accompaniments:

Noodles - Cook thin egg noodles until tender. Rinse with cold water, drain. Place a large spoonful of noodles in each bowl, and then pour the soup.

Rice - Cook 1/4 cup raw rice for 10 servings of soup. Use like the noodles.

Mandlen - Available in markets; heat in a 350° oven for 5 minutes. Store in a jar. Add to the bowls before serving.

Knaidlach - 3 large eggs
1 tablespoon water
2 tablespoons chicken fat
1 teaspoon salt
Freshly ground pepper to taste
1/2 cup matzo meal

continued

Blend all ingredients thoroughly. Cover and refrigerate 3 hours. Bring a large pot of salted water to a boil. Wet your hands; shape the batter into balls 1 inch in diameter. Drop them gently (do not crowd!) into the boiling water. Turn the heat to medium and cook for 30 minutes. The knaidlach will sink to the bottom, then rise to the top. Using a slotted spoon, remove them from the pot to a bowl. Gently place the knaidlach in the soup when it is lukewarm. This recipe makes enough knaidlach for 8 servings.

BEAN AND BARLEY SOUP

2 cups dried lima beans
3 pounds flanken (lean short ribs)
Several marrow bones
3 1/4 quarts water
1/4 cup pearl barley
3 chopped onions
2 crushed garlic cloves
1 chopped carrot
Freshly ground pepper
1 handful chopped parsley

Soak the dried lima beans in water overnight; drain. Put the meat and bones in a large pot. Add the water; bring to a boil. Skim; lower the heat. Simmer for 1 hour. Add the barley, onions, carrot, and lima beans; cook for 2 hours. Add the remaining ingredients. Continue cooking for 20 minutes until everything is tender. Remove the bones from the soup and allow to cool; refrigerate overnight. Remove the surface fat. Heat slowly; season and serve.

COLD CABBAGE BORSCHT

1 small head cabbage, shredded
1 pint sour cream at room temperature
Lemon juice
Salt
Freshly ground pepper

Cook the cabbage in boiling salted water until it is just tender. Cool; drain the cabbage, reserving the liquid. Whisk the cabbage liquid and the sour cream until smooth. Add the cabbage and season with lemon juice, salt, and pepper. Add a little sugar if it is too tart. Chill. Serves 4.

SPEEDY BEET BORSCHT

1 can (1-pound) diced beets
1 1/2 cups sour cream at room temperature
Juice of 1 lemon
Salt
Freshly ground pepper to taste

Drain the beets; reserve the liquid. Add the liquid to the sour cream until smooth. Add the beets and lemon juice. Adjust the seasoning. Serve with a sour cream garnish sprinkled with fresh or dried dill. Serves 4.

BUBELE'S BEAN BORSCHT

1/2 pound fresh green beans, cut into 2-inch lengths
1 1/2 cups sour cream at room temperature
Lemon juice
Salt and pepper

Cook fresh green beans in boiling salted water in an uncovered pot until they are just tender. Cool. Reserve the liquid. Whisk the sour cream and bean liquid together until smooth. Add the beans; season to taste with the lemon juice, salt, and pepper. Serve chilled or at room temperature. This makes 4 servings.

TOMATO SOUP

2 cans (No. 2 1/2) tomatoes
1 can (8 -ounce) tomato sauce
1 pound chicken backs and necks
1 clove garlic
1 peeled potato
2 stalks celery
1 peeled onion
1 handful of chopped parsley
Salt, pepper, paprika, fines herbes

Wash the chicken parts. Drain and rinse them. Place all the ingredients except the seasonings in a large pot. Add water to 1 inch from the top of the pot. Season the soup. Bring to a boil and skim. Simmer for 2 1/2 hours half covered. Re-season to taste. Strain the soup; serve with cooked rice.

SPLIT-PEA SOUP

Like most soups, this soup is better the next day - after the seasonings have been allowed to amalgamate.

2 1/2 quarts water
1 3/4 cups green split peas
2 1/2 pounds flanken (lean short ribs)
Several large marrow bones
2 1/2 teaspoons salt
Freshly ground pepper
2 peeled and grated carrots
2 chopped onions

Wash the split peas; drain and rinse. Bring the peas and water to a boil in a large pot. Simmer for 1 hour. Wash the bones; add the remaining ingredients to the pot. Cover and cook for 3 hours or until the meat is tender. Serve unstrained or pureed, having first removed the meat and bones. Freezes well. Heat and season before serving.

YENTA'S LENTIL SOUP

Without a ham bone yet!

1 3/4 cups lentils
8 1/2 cups water
3 chopped onions
2 1/2 tablespoons chicken fat
2 chopped carrots
1 tablespoon salt
1 bay leaf
Freshly ground pepper
3 sliced kosher knockwurst

Wash the lentils. Put the lentils and water into a large soup pot. Bring to a boil, stirring occasionally. Lower the heat and simmer for 1 hour. Saute the chopped onions in the fat until brown. Add the onions and the remaining ingredients (except the knockwurst) to the lentils. Simmer for 2 hours. Remove the bay leaf. Serve unstrained. Heat before serving; re-season; add the knockwurst 10 minutes before serving.

KIBBUTZ
SHEPHERD

Salads

Salads are virtually the 'unknown soldiers' of the Jewish menu. There are a few old favorites which even Bubbeleh made, and which are represented here in two versions of cole slaw: one creamy and one with vinegar and oil. Sweet and sour cucumbers were the traditional salad, with plenty of onions, and when fish was served we enjoyed a creamy version. Here are some of the old timers.

And here is also a modern salad direct from Israel. This Kibbutznick Salad is great for breakfast, is really a complete lunch, and we were delighted to find it representing the new 'green' nation.

COLE SLAW

For crisp, crunchy vegetables, prepare not more than an hour before serving.

1 head cabbage - about 2 pounds
2 shredded carrots
1 thinly sliced green pepper
1/4 cup plumped raisins
1/4 cup water
1/2 cup cider vinegar
1/2 cup mayonnaise
1 tablespoon sugar
2 teaspoons salt
Freshly ground pepper
1/2 teaspoon celery seed
1 tablespoon white horseradish

Shred the cabbage. Add the carrots, green pepper, and raisins. Whisk the remaining ingredients together in a bowl. Pour over the vegetables; mix thoroughly. Refrigerate.

COLE SLAW VINAIGRETTE

1 small shredded head cabbage
1 diced green pepper
2 grated carrots
1 teaspoon salt
1/2 teaspoon dry mustard
3/4 teaspoon celery salt
2 tablespoons sugar
1 chopped pimento
2 teaspoons grated onion
3 tablespoons oil (not olive oil)
1/3 cup white vinegar
Freshly ground pepper

Combine the vegetables. Whisk together the remaining ingredients. Pour over the vegetables, mixing thoroughly. Refrigerate. Prepare the day before so the flavors will blend. This salad looks pretty in a glass bowl. Serve at room temperature.

THE BALABOOSTA'S POTATO SALAD

For best results, prepare this dish not more than 4 hours before serving.

8 waxy potatoes (red or Shafter)
1 bunch minced parsley
1 bunch minced green onions
Salt and pepper
1/4 cup defatted beef or poultry juice
White wine vinegar to taste
Pinch sugar
Paprika

Use uniform-sized potatoes. Bring to a boil in salted water, and simmer just until tender, about 15 to 30 minutes. Peel the hot potatoes. Sprinkle them with vinegar and the meat juice. Add the rest of the ingredients. Toss gently. Garnish with paprika. Serve at room temperature. Serves 6 to 8.

KIBBUTZNICK SALAD

2 cucumbers
1 bunch radishes
1 bunch green onions
1 sliced green pepper
2 diced tomatoes
1 1/2 pints cottage cheese
1 pint sour cream

Peel and quarter the cucumbers lengthwise. Seed and cut them into 1-inch chunks. Clean and trim the radishes. Wash, trim, and cut the onions into 1-inch pieces. Serve everything separately — buffet style. Delicious with freshly baked rye bread and butter. Serves 4 to 6.

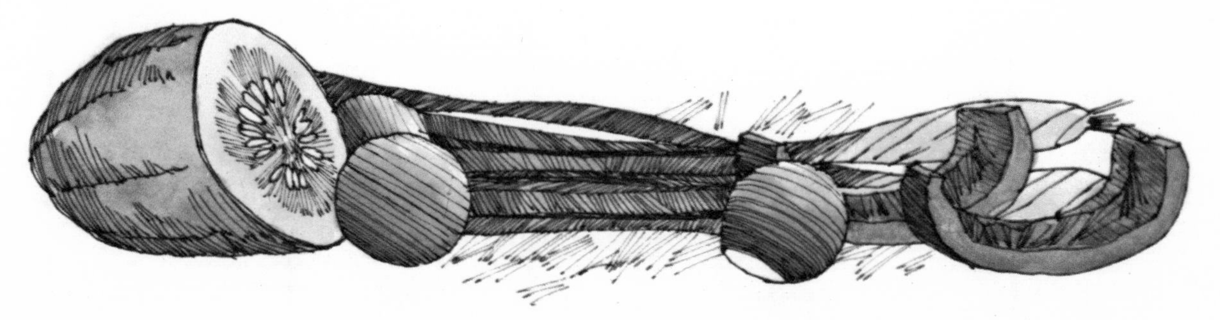

CUCUMBER SALAD

4 peeled and sliced cucumbers
1 cup white vinegar
3/4 cup sugar
1/2 cup water
Fresh or dried dill
1 small onion, sliced paper-thin

Put the cucumber and onion slices in a glass bowl. Combine the remaining ingredients in a saucepan. Bring to a boil; pour over the cucumber and onion slices. Refrigerate. Prepare on the same day it is to be served. Serve in small individual bowls.

CREAMY VARIATION: Drain the cucumbers and onions, reserving the marinade. Whisk 3/4 cup sour cream with 1/4 cup marinade. Add to the cucumbers and season with salt, pepper, and paprika. Chill. Serve.

CHOPPED EGGS AND ONIONS

6 hard-boiled eggs
1/2 cup minced onions
Salt to taste
Freshly ground pepper to taste
2 tablespoons chicken fat at room temperature

Chop the eggs and onions on a wooden chopping block, using a chef's knife. When mixture is well chopped, transfer to a bowl. Season to taste, adding the fat to bind mixture together.

Serve as a salad on lettuce, as a matzo spread, or as a filling for sandwiches. Enough for 6 salads or sandwiches, or for 12 as a spread.

ST. SIMON
SOUVENIRS
SHOP
NAJARIAN'S
ORIENTAL
STORE

Jewish-Style Vegetables

Vegetables are usually served at Jewish meals but are rarely the outstanding feature. Creamed Mushrooms Kolta is a prominent exception to this. It was always a very special treat because Grandma used $8-a-pound dried mushrooms from New York, and they were a mechaieh. Try it with Czech mushrooms if you possibly can.

Baked beans are served with delicatessen-type entrees such as corned beef or tongue. The results of this recipe will spoil you for canned baked beans forever.

Red Cabbage, Sweet and Sour, is a foil for Brust, as well as duck or goose. Haimische Vegetable Tzimmes is the one dish in this section which we eat at almost every holiday meal. Its sauce and lilting flavor typify the vegetable, Jewish gourmet style.

SWEET AND SOUR GREEN BEANS

1 pound cooked green beans, cut into 2-inch pieces, drained (reserve liquid)
1 tablespoon chicken fat
1 heaping tablespoon flour
1 teaspoon white vinegar
1 tablespoon sugar

Melt the fat in a skillet. Add the flour, stirring constantly, until it is a deep tan. Carefully add some of the bean liquid, whisking constantly. When it thickens, add more liquid, continuing to stir. Add the vinegar; mix well. Add to the beans in a saucepan. Simmer. Add the sugar. Adjust the flavor, adding either more vinegar or sugar. Serve hot in individual bowls. Serves 6.

SWEET AND SOUR LENTILS: Use above recipe, substituting 1 pound dry lentils for the beans. Cook as directed on the package.

GRANDMA'S BAKED BEANS

1 pound dried baby lima beans, cooked and drained
1 1/4 cups tomato juice
1/4 cup catsup
1 cup tomato puree
3/4 cup brown sugar
Salt and pepper
2 teaspoons hot mustard or horseradish
1/2 pound homemade pickled brisket (a fatty part)

Place 1 cup tomato juice, catsup, puree, sugar, salt and pepper in a 2-quart bean pot and simmer until the sugar dissolves. Add the mustard (or horseradish) and mix well. Cut the meat into julienne strips. Layer the beans, meat, and tomato sauce. Cover the pan tightly; bake for 2 hours in a 325° oven. Remove the pot from the oven, uncover, and cool. Refrigerate overnight. Mix in the remaining tomato juice. Cover and bake at 325° for 1 hour. Serves 6.

SWEET AND SOUR RED CABBAGE

1 small shredded red cabbage
Boiling water
1 tablespoon chicken fat
1 large green apple, peeled, cored, diced
1 cup water
1/4 cup red wine vinegar
1 tablespoon sugar
Salt and pepper to taste
1 tablespoon chicken fat
1 tablespoon granulated flour
1/4 cup raisins soaked overnight
in sweet Jewish wine
1/4 cup cooked, diced chestnuts

Wilt the cabbage with boiling water. Drain; dry in paper towels. Saute the cabbage and apple in fat for 10 minutes. Add water, vinegar, sugar, and seasonings. After it boils, cover and cook until tender (20 minutes). Brown the flour, stirring constantly. Whisk in cabbage liquid until smooth. Add cabbage; simmer for 10 minutes. Add raisins and chestnuts. Adjust seasoning. Serves 6.

HAIMISCHE VEGETABLE TZIMMES

2 pounds carrots, peeled
1 pound fresh, shelled peas
3 sweet potatoes, peeled, quartered
1 teaspoon sugar
1/2 teaspoon salt
Freshly ground pepper
1 teaspoon brown sugar
1 tablespoon chicken fat
1 tablespoon granulated flour

Slice the carrots 1/2 inch thick crosswise. Add the peas; set aside. Cover the potatoes with water; bring to a boil. Simmer uncovered for 15 minutes, or until partly done. Add the carrots and peas to the potatoes. Add water to cover the vegetables, and the seasonings. Cook for 10 minutes; add the sauce and simmer for 10 minutes. Serve hot in small individual bowls. Serves 8.

CREAMED MUSHROOMS KOLTA

2 ounces dried mushrooms
Salt
1 pound fresh, sliced button mushrooms
2 tablespoons butter
2 minced onions
2 cups sour cream
1 heaping tablespoon flour
1 tablespoon lemon juice
1 large egg

Buy the Czech-dried mushrooms or half Italian, half Japanese. Wash them, changing the water several times. Cover them with water in a pot. Add a pinch of salt; bring to a boil. Cover, and simmer for 45 minutes. Remove the mushrooms from the cooking liquid. Slice them; strain and reserve the liquid. Cover the fresh mushrooms with water in a pot. Bring to a boil, cover, and simmer for 10 minutes. Remove them from their broth; add to the other mushrooms. Saute the onions until golden. Dice the cooked dried mushrooms. Combine the remaining ingredients with a whisk. This is the critical part. Slowly heat the cream mixture, whisking constantly. Have half the mushroom broth in a bowl and half in a pan. Gradually add some of the broth to the cream mixture, beating very hard with the whisk. Pour the cream mixture into the broth in the pot, whisking constantly. Slowly heat this. Add any remaining broth, whisking for all you are worth. NEVER, NEVER LET THIS MIXTURE BOIL! Best served cold. Serves 8 or more if used as a sauce.

PART OF 18th CENTURY WALL
AND FISHERMAN HARBOUR

Blintzes

A blintze is a "thin pancake folded or rolled around a filling, as of cheese or fruit, and fried in oil or butter, or baked," according to the dictionary. The Russians adorn it with sour cream and caviar, and the Italians fill it with a meat mixture and top it with cheese. There are as many ways to prepare blintzes as you can imagine, so think up your own original ways of preparing them: in any language – with any filling – they are delicious.

The classic blintze is folded, as described in the following pages. However, you can roll your blintzes around the filling just as easily, and this method is better when you want to use more than just a dollop of filling.

Blintzes are served for breakfast, lunch, or dinner – at any time of the day and, depending on the filling, can be used as an appetizer, an entree, or dessert. An elegant dish, its preparation is simplicity itself.

BLINTZES

Use a French black iron crepe pan, No. 18. First scrub it with a soapy wire pad. Dry well; pour 1 inch of corn oil into it. Place it in a 300° oven. Turn the oven off after 2 hours. Leave the pan in the oven 12 hours longer. Pour off the oil and discard it. Wipe the pan thoroughly with paper towels until no trace of oil remains. Your pan is now "seasoned." This acts like a teflon finish. When you are finished using the pan, never, NEVER, wash it. Wipe it with paper towels until it is grease-free. Use it only for blintzes.

BATTER

1 1/8 cups granulated flour
1/8 teaspoon salt
3 large eggs
1 1/2 cups milk
2 tablespoons corn oil
Butter

Beat the eggs, salt, and milk together until foamy. Add the flour and whisk until smooth. Add the oil and refrigerate for 1 hour. Pour 1 teaspoon of oil into the pan with 1/2 teaspoon butter. Place the pan on medium-high heat; wait until the fat sizzles. Ladle just enough batter into the pan so that the surface of the pan is barely covered when you rotate it. Replace the pan on the heat until the top of the crepe appears "set," not liquid. On an electric range rotate the pan several times for even heat. Turn the crepe, cook on the second side for 30 seconds. This will be the outside of the blintze. Remove to a foil-lined counter. Add another sliver of butter to the pan and repeat the procedure until no more batter remains. Makes 18 to 20 pancakes. Keep them in a single layer. Use 2 tablespoons filling for each blintze.

FILLING THE BLINTZE:

Fill and roll the traditional blintzes according to the drawings and keep hot in oven before serving. OR: The blintzes can be cooled and frozen with foil between the layers. To reheat, bake them in a single layer on a greased cooky sheet for 15 minutes in a 375° oven. They must be very hot. Serve with sour cream, jams, and fresh fruit. Serve as hors d'oeuvres, main course, or dessert.

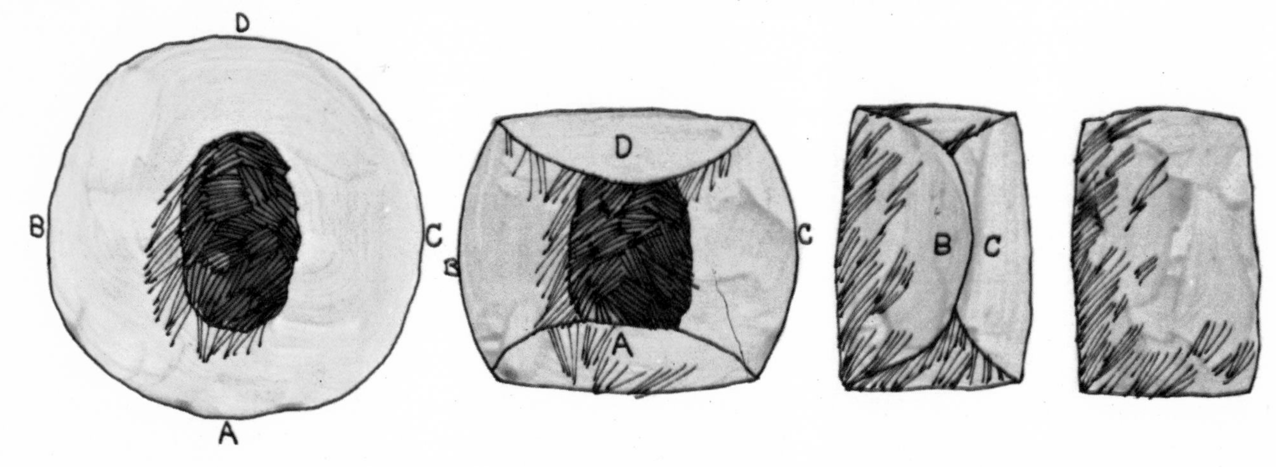

RICH DESSERT FILLING

3 tablespoons white raisins
1 1/2 tablespoons cognac
12 ounces softened cream cheese
6 tablespoons sugar
1 1/2 tablespoons granulated flour
2 egg yolks
1 1/2 teaspoons melted butter
1 1/2 tablespoons sour cream
Grated rind of 1 large lemon
3/4 teaspoon vanilla

Marinate the raisins in cognac 8 hours. Mix the cream cheese, sugar, and flour together until fluffy. Add the remaining ingredients except the raisins and mix well. Add the raisins, mix, and chill. This filling is very rich and perfect for dessert.

TRADITONAL CHEESE FILLING

1 1/4 pounds farmer cheese
5 ounces softened cream cheese
2 1/2 tablespoons soft butter
1/3 cup + 1 1/2 tablespoons sugar

Mix ingredients until smooth and creamy. Chill.

SALMON-MUSHROOM FILLING

Cream Sauce:
1 cup butter
1 cup granulated flour
White pepper to taste
2 teaspoons salt
Paprika
1 quart light cream or half-and-half

Melt the butter over medium heat. Sprinkle the flour over the butter, whisking constantly. When smooth, season it, and add the cream. Whisk constantly until thickened. Remove from the heat. Cover the surface of the sauce with waxed paper. Set aside.

Filling:

1/2 cup butter
1 tablespoon oil
4 diced large onions
1 pound sliced mushrooms
1 finely diced green pepper
2 1/2 pounds cold, cooked salmon
Salt, white pepper, fines herbes
Tabasco, dill

Saute the onions until limp. Add the mushrooms and green pepper. Continue cooking until the onions brown and the mushrooms and green pepper are tender. Remove from the heat. Skin, bone, and flake the salmon. Add to the onions. Add this mixture to the cream sauce. Season to taste. Chill, and use within a day. This is better if not frozen.

MEAT FILLING

Prepare Hungarian gulyas (page 91). Drain the gravy. Bring to a boil; reduce the volume to half. Add to the meat. Chill and remove surface fat.

A SHEPHERD AND HIS
GOATS OUTSIDE THE WALLS
OF JERUSALEM

Noodles and Other Good Things

Egg noodles are a favorite Jewish dish: in soup, in kugel, served with the main dish, or as a main dish. My grandmother prepared her own special noodle dough. It was rolled, cut, dried, and stored in glass jars. The very finely cut noodles were reserved for chicken soup. A special treat was farfel, tiny dot-shaped pieces of egg barley for which we include a delicious, easy recipe.

The noodle recipe is included specifically for kreplach. Otherwise you can purchase every kind of pasta in the supermarket, delicatessen, or Italian market. Be sure to cook them properly, using plenty of boiling, salted water. Never overcook.

I associate potatoes, galuska, latkes, and chremsels, to name a few, with noodles. These are the backbone of the Jewish meal. Eat them by themselves or with a main course. You should have much mazel with these recipes.

KREPLACH

Kreplach, won ton, and ravioli are cousins under the skin.

3 cups all-purpose flour
4 large eggs
1 tablespoon salt

Place the flour in a bowl. Make a well in the center. Add the eggs and salt to the well. Knead with your hands until very smooth and quite elastic. Add a few drops of water at a time, if necessary. The dough should be rolled, cut, and filled immediately. Roll it, one part at a time, as thin as possible, about 1/8 inch thick. Lean on the rolling pin because the dough is elastic. Cut into 3-inch squares. Fill according to the diagram. Brush the edges of the square with a little water before you fold it. After it is formed, crimp the edges with a fork. Boil a 6-quart pot of salted water. Gently lower the kreplach into the boiling water, using a slotted spoon; cook them for 20 minutes or until they rise to the surface. Drain. Repeat the procedure with the rest of the dough and filling. Serve in soup, as a main dish, or as a side dish. These can be deep fried or baked, basted with fat and sprinkled with bread crumbs. Makes 36 kreplach.

Beef Filling:

3/4 pound boneless steak
1 1/2 tablespoons chicken fat
2 large chopped onions
2 crushed garlic cloves
Salt and pepper to taste

Broil the steak; cool. Saute the onions until well brown. Add the garlic; mix well. Trim all the fat from the steak. Grind the meat using the finest blade. Combine all the ingredients. Season to taste. Chill until used.

continued

Chicken:	3 tablespoons chicken fat	2 1/4 cups ground, cooked chicken
	2 large grated onions	2 large egg yolks
	1 minced garlic clove	Salt and pepper to taste
	1/4 cup grated green pepper	2 tablespoons minced parsley

Saute the onions and garlic until well browned. Add the green pepper about halfway through. Combine with the chicken and remaining ingredients. If it is too dry, add half of another egg yolk. Season well. Chill.

Liver Filling:	3/4 pound beef liver	Salt and pepper
	2 large chopped onions	Pinch of sugar
	3 tablespoons chicken fat	Dash of Tabasco sauce
	3 hard-boiled egg yolks	

Broil the beef liver. Saute the onions until quite brown. Grind the liver, onions, and egg yolks, using the finest blade. Add the remaining ingredients. Season well. Chill.

Kasha Filling:

- 1/4 cup chicken fat
- 2 large minced onions
- 1/2 pound chopped mushrooms
- 2 cups cooked kasha
- 2 tablespoons minced parsley
- Salt and pepper to taste

Saute the chopped green onions until tender. Add the rest of the ingredients except the seasonings. Mix thoroughly. Season well. Serve with sour cream as a part of a dairy meal, either as a side dish or as the main course.

NOODLES

Fill a 6-quart pot two-thirds full of salted water. Bring to a boil. Add 12 ounces of noodles. Cook, uncovered, stirring frequently. Turn the heat to simmer when the water resumes boiling. Check the noodles by tasting. Eat immediately, or keep hot in the top of a double boiler over boiling water. Makes 8 servings.

VARIATIONS

BUTTER: The simplest way to serve noodles is with lots of butter, seasoned with salt, pepper, and paprika.

POPPYSEED: Add 1/4 cup poppyseed to the buttered noodles. Season with salt, white pepper, and paprika. Garnish with parsley.

RAISINS: For the sweet tooth, add 1/4 cup plumped raisins to the buttered noodles. Sprinkle with a mixture of 1/4 cup sugar mixed with 1 tablespoon cinnamon and 2 tablespoons grated almonds. Delicious with everything!

ONIONS: Saute 3 large chopped onions and 2 cloves of crushed garlic in chicken fat until brown. Add to the noodles. Serve immediately after seasoning with salt, pepper, and fines herbes, or keep warm in a double boiler.

CHEESE: I once ate this daily at lunch for a week! Add 1/2 pound of fresh farmer cheese, broken into small chunks, to the hot buttered noodles. Season with salt. pepper, and paprika. Serve immediately. Top each serving with sour cream. Cottage cheese or 6 ounces cream cheese can be substituted for farmer cheese. For variety add chopped green onions.

PISCKOS TESTA: Mix lekvar (imported plum jam) and cinnamon with the noodles.

NOODLES AND CABBAGE

Chicken fat
3 large minced onions
1 shredded head cabbage
Salt and pepper to taste
Pinch sugar
12 ounces cooked wide egg noodles

Saute the onions until soft; add the cabbage. Season with the sugar, salt, and pepper. Add more chicken fat, if necessary, until the cabbage and onions are brown. Add the noodles. Correct the seasoning and serve. Tastes best with boldly seasoned foods. Serves 8 to 10.

KASHA

Kasha, roasted buckwheat groats, is a favored filling for knishes, derma, helzel, and poultry. Here are two typically Jewish recipes for it.

3 tablespoons chicken fat
1 cup kasha
1 large beaten egg
1 heaping teaspoon paprika
1 small minced onion
2 1/2 cups chicken stock

Saute the kasha until coated with the fat. Add the remaining ingredients, stirring after each. Bring to a boil; cover. Simmer for 15 minutes, until most of the stock has been absorbed. Uncover and place in a 350° oven for 20 minutes. The kasha will be lightly browned. Serves 4 generously. Garnish with chopped parsley.

KASHA WITH VARNISHKES

Kasha can be served in place of potatoes or rice. The mishpocheh will rave!

1 recipe of kasha, cooked with 3 minced cloves garlic
8 ounces bowties, cooked (a variety of noodle)
Salt and pepper to taste

Combine the hot kasha with the cooked and well drained bowties (varnishkes). Season to taste with salt and pepper. This should never be bland.

FARFEL

Serve farfel (egg barley) in soup or with meat.

1/4 cup chicken fat
1 minced onion
2 crushed garlic cloves
1/4 pound chopped mushrooms
1/2 small chopped green pepper
2 cups uncooked farfel
Salt and pepper to taste
3 cups boiling chicken or beef stock

Saute the onions, garlic, and mushrooms in a 4-quart casserole until soft. Add the green pepper; cook until soft. Season with salt and pepper. Add the boiling stock, and cover the casserole. Place in a 350° oven for 45 minutes. This will keep in the oven for 15 minutes. Serves 8 to 10.

THE KUGEL WITH TAM

Better than a potato, great for dessert, and delicious with ice cream!

12 ounces wide egg noodles
1 large egg + 1 egg yolk
1/4 cup plumped raisins
Cinnamon
1/4 cup sugar
1 can (No. 303) applesauce
Vegetable shortening

Fill a 6-quart pot with 4 quarts of salted water. Bring to a boil. Add the noodles. When the water resumes boiling, lower the heat to medium, stirring frequently. Eat one to test when just done (about 10 minutes). Drain, run cold water over them, and drain well. Place them in a large bowl. Mix the sugar with enough cinnamon so the mixture is a rich brown. Beat the egg and yolk until frothy. Add the beaten eggs, cinnamon, sugar, and raisins to the noodles. Mix well. Heat 1-1/2 tablespoons vegetable shortening in a 9x9x2-inch metal baking pan in a 350° oven. When the shortening is melted remove the pan from the oven. Arrange half the noodles in the pan in an even layer. Spread the applesauce over this. Carefully spoon the remaining noodles over the applesauce. Dot the top with 2 tablespoons vegetable shortening cut into small pieces. Bake in a 350° oven for 1 hour, until the noodles on top are crisp and brown. Cut and serve while hot. Cool and refrigerate overnight. Cut into portions; wrap them individually in foil. Place them in a tightly closed plastic bag. Freeze. To serve, thaw at room temperature at least 4 hours. Reheat on a cooky sheet (still wrapped in foil) in a 350° oven for 25 to 35 minutes. Serves 8 to 10.

POTATO KUGEL

Whether crisp and crunchy or delicately soft, kugel is essential to a meal featuring a meat entree.

1/3 cup potato starch
1/2 teaspoon baking powder
Salt and pepper
1 large grated onion
3 large beaten eggs
1/4 cup melted chicken fat
3 cups grated potatoes
Chicken fat

Mix potato starch, baking powder, salt and pepper. Add the remaining ingredients except the unmelted chicken fat. Turn into a 2-quart casserole, well greased with chicken fat. Bake in a 375° oven for 1 hour, until the top is very brown and crusty. Serves 6.

BRING-ALONG NOODLE PUDDING

1 pound wide egg noodles
4 large eggs + 1 egg yolk
Pinch salt
1/2 cup sugar
1 cup sour cream
2 3/4 cups milk
Juice of 1/2 lemon
1 teaspoon vanilla
1 1/8 cups corn flakes
1/2 cup melted butter

Grease a 13x9x2-inch glass baking pan with vegetable shortening. Beat the eggs and yolk with the salt and sugar until light colored and creamy. Add the sour cream, milk, lemon juice, and vanilla with a whisk until smooth. Add the noodles to this and blend gently but thoroughly. Pour the noodle mixture into the pan in an even layer. Crush the cornflakes in your hand; mix with the melted butter. Spoon mixture evenly over the top of the noodles. Bake in a 375° oven for 1 hour until golden brown (400° in a metal pan). Tastes best when eaten while hot. Do not freeze; prepare ahead and refrigerate before reheating. Serves 10 to 12.

GALUSKA

3 cups sifted all-purpose flour
2 large eggs
1 teaspoon salt
3/4 cup water
2 teaspoons chicken fat

Beat the flour, eggs, salt, and 3/4 cup water in an electric mixer on medium speed until small bubbles appear on the surface. Bring 4 quarts of salted water to a boil. Using 2 teaspoons, fill one with dough and drop small pieces into the water by pushing the dough off with the second spoon. This dough expands quite a bit. Galuska are not good when large. After all the dough has been used, continue to cook for 5 more minutes. Drain well; turn into a serving dish with the fat or butter. Toss the galuska so that all are coated with the fat. Serve with some gravy. (Can be kept warm in the covered top of a double boiler over simmering water not more than 20 minutes.) Serves 6.

TZIBBELE POTATOES

This dish combines two staples in Jewish cooking - and what tam!

3 large chopped onions
1/4 cup chicken fat
Salt and pepper
8 hot, cooked potatoes

Saute the onions until they are golden with lovely dark brown edges. Season with salt and pepper. Mash the potatoes in a bowl; add the onions. Adjust the seasoning. If the dish is too dry add some chicken fat. Serves 5 to 6.

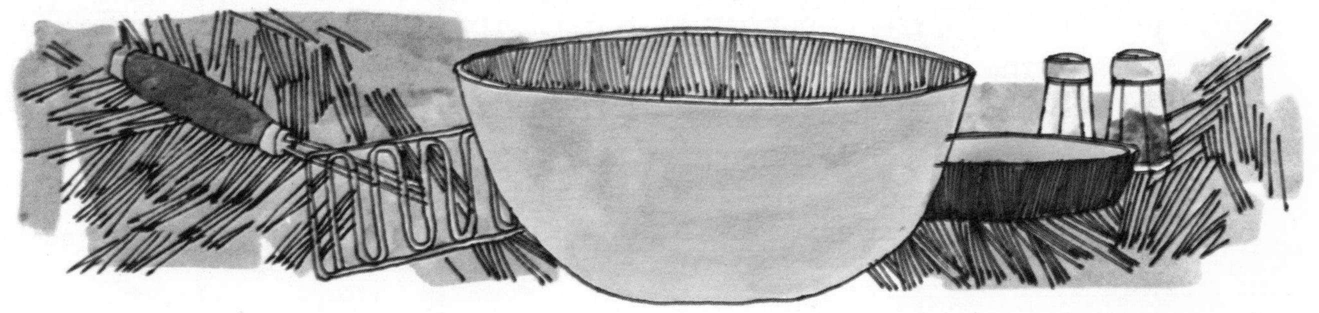

LATKES WITH CHUTZPAH

2 large eggs + 1 egg yolk
2 small grated onions
1/4 cup minced parsley
2 tablespoons granulated flour
1/4 heaping teaspoon baking powder
4 medium shredded potatoes
Salt and pepper
1/3 cup chicken fat

Beat the eggs and yolk and add the remaining ingredients, except the fat, to the eggs. Shred the potatoes just before adding them. It will look very peculiar. Be certain it is well seasoned. Heat the fat in a large heavy skillet over medium-high heat (or use an electric frying pan set at 400°). Drop the potato mixture from a large spoon into the hot fat, creating mounds 3 inches in diameter. Flatten them with the turner. Occasionally press the latke into the fat so that it will brown evenly. Turn carefully when the underside is brown and crusty. Brown the second side. Remove from the pan and drain on paper towels. Keep warm in a 350° oven in a single layer for no more than 20 minutes. Serve piping hot with applesauce or sour cream.

CHREMSELS

- 4 egg yolks
- 1/2 teaspoon salt
- 1/2 cup cold water
- Grated rind of a lemon
- 3/4 cup matzo meal
- 3 stiffly beaten egg whites
- Oil or homogenized shortening

Beat the egg yolks, salt, water, and lemon rind together. Add the matzo meal, keeping the mixture smooth. Gently fold in the egg whites. Heat the fat to 375° in a large heavy skillet. Drop the batter from a tablespoon into the hot fat. The chremsels should be well browned on both sides. Drain on paper towels. Eat immediately. Serve with the meal as a side dish or as the main course.

VARIATIONS: If serving chremsels with meat, substitute 2 tablespoons chopped parsley or grated onion for the lemon rind. Season with salt and pepper.

BEDOUIN WOMAN WITH
WATER JAR

Meat

Religious dietary laws have limited both the variety of meat and the cuts available to the Jewish cook. Within this range, however, is a whole gamut of foods, from Halushkes to Chopped Lung, Stuffed Breast of Veal to Sweet and Sour Tongue. The mark that especially distinguishes Jewish cooking is the seasoning. Onions, garlic, and salt, pepper, and paprika are generously used, but you must taste the foods you are cooking in order to properly season them. Perhaps that accounts for the zoftig Jewish cook. Once you have tasted the Roast Chicken or the Yiddish Mama's Turkey you will be spoiled by it. No more bland food for you. Tam, tam, tam.

CHICKEN PAPRIKASH

Feed this haimische dish to a Landsman.

1/4 cup chicken fat
3 large chopped onions
1 chicken (4-pound) sectioned
2 tablespoons Hungarian sweet paprika
Salt
1 thinly sliced green pepper
1 large peeled, seeded, diced tomato
1 teaspoon tomato paste

Saute the onions in a 4-quart pot until golden brown. Lower the heat to medium; add the chicken, paprika, and 1 teaspoon salt. Cover and simmer for 10 minutes. Stir several times, adding a little water only if necessary. Add the green pepper, tomato, tomato paste, and 1 cup water. Cover the pan. Simmer about 50 minutes, stirring and adding water if needed to prevent the food from sticking to the pan. Adjust the seasoning. Serves 4. Perfect with galuska.

MAMA'S ROAST CHICKEN

1 chicken
Salt, pepper, paprika
1 whole onion
2 garlic cloves grated with 1 onion
1 bay leaf
1/2 cup canned tomatoes

Wash and dry the chicken thoroughly, including the cavity. Rub salt, pepper, and paprika all over the skin, including the cavity. Place the whole onion inside the chicken. Apply a liberal coating of onion and garlic all over the chicken. Pour 2 cups water, the bay leaf, and the canned tomatoes in the bottom of a small roaster. Place the chicken on a rack in the pan. Roast, uncovered, in a 450° oven until the chicken starts to sizzle, then reduce the temperature to 400°. Cover the roaster with heavy foil. Baste the chicken occasionally with the juices on the pan bottom. Add water to these juices only when needed. Roast the bird at 400° for 1 hour. Lower the heat to 375° for 30 minutes longer. Turn the chicken from time to time to cook evenly. Pierce the inside of the thigh with a fork. If it is done the juices should run clear and the fork exit easily. Serves 4.

GRANDMA'S CHICKEN FRICASSEE

2 cans (8-ounce) tomato sauce with bits
1 can (No. 303) tomatoes
3 diced onions
2 diced celery stalks
2 bay leaves
3 minced cloves garlic
1 diced green pepper
Salt, pepper, paprika
3 pounds chicken legs and wings
1 pound lean ground beef
1 large egg
1 medium grated onion
1/2 cup raw rice

Use 2 heavy pots for this dish. The chicken takes less time to cook than the meat and each needs room to cook. They are combined when done and served together.

Pour 4 cups water into a pot. Add 1 can tomato sauce, 1/2 can tomatoes, half the diced onions, half the celery, 1 bay leaf, half of the minced garlic, and half the green pepper. Season with 1 teaspoon salt, 1/4 teaspoon pepper, and paprika. Bring to a boil, then lower the heat. Add the chicken, stir, taste and season. Simmer 1 hour until chicken is tender, turning occasionally. When done remove from heat.

Add the egg, salt, pepper, paprika, grated onion, and rice to the ground beef. Mix together gently but thoroughly. Form into balls the size of a large walnut. Prepare the gravy as noted with the chicken, using the remaining ingredients. Bring to a boil and lower the heat to a simmer. Add the meat balls and cook for 1 1/2 hours, stirring occasionally.

Remove the bay leaves from both pots. Combine the chicken, meat balls, and gravy. Generously serves 6 to 8.

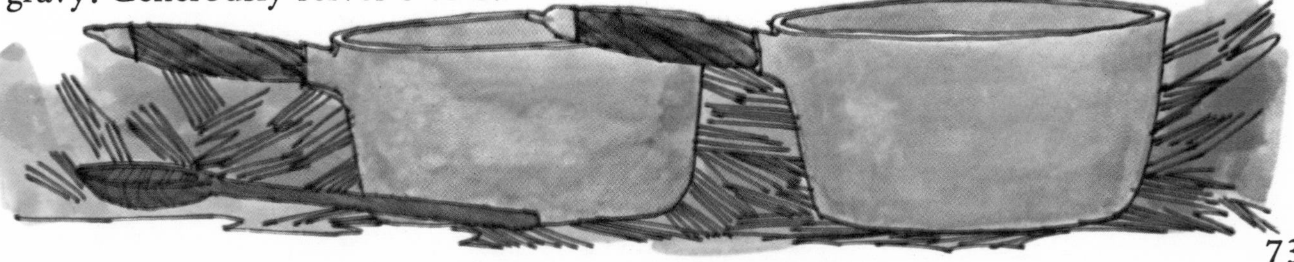

OUR GERMAN SUPPER

Perfect when the gelt is scarce, this dish takes only 25 minutes to prepare.

2 tablespoons chicken fat
3 large diced onions
1 can (No. 2 1/2) sauerkraut
6 large cooked cold potatoes
6 knockwurst
Salt and pepper

Saute the onions until brown. Drain the sauerkraut and rinse several times with water to remove the strong taste of brine. Peel and quarter the potatoes. Add them with the sauerkraut to the onions. Season lightly. Simmer for 15 minutes until everything is hot. Lay the knockwurst on top of the skillet; cover it. They will release their tasty juices into the sauerkraut-potato mixture. Season lightly. Served with plenty of mustards and thickly sliced rye bread, it is plenty for 6. Beer is the perfect thirst-quencher.

HALUSHKES

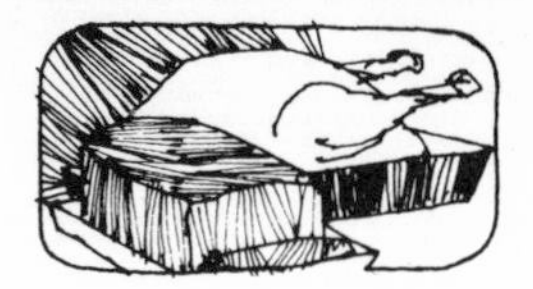

This dollar-stretching gourmet treat is an all-time favorite at our house.

1 large head cabbage
1 pound ground chuck
6 tablespoons raw rice
1 grated onion
2 large eggs
1 teaspoon salt
Ground pepper

2 cans (8 ounces) tomato sauce with bits
2 cans (No. 2 1/2) tomatoes
Juice of 2 lemons
1 teaspoon salt
Ground pepper
1/2 cup brown sugar

Place the cabbage in a large pot of boiling water. Leave it in the water long enough to soften the outer leaves. The color changes a little and you can see the cabbage is softer. Lift the cabbage from the water. Remove the softened leaves cutting them away at the base of the core. Replace the cabbage in the pot and repeat the process until all the leaves are softened. Drain them. Trim the rib on the base of the leaf with a vegetable peeler so it is the same thickness as the rest of the leaf.

Cook the rice until it is thoroughly soft; let it cool. Combine the cooked rice, ground chuck, onion, eggs, salt and pepper. Line the bottom of a 6-quart pot with the tiny cabbage leaves and any torn ones. (Refer to the drawings to fill and roll the leaves.) Adjust the amount of filling to the size of the leaf. Layer the stuffed

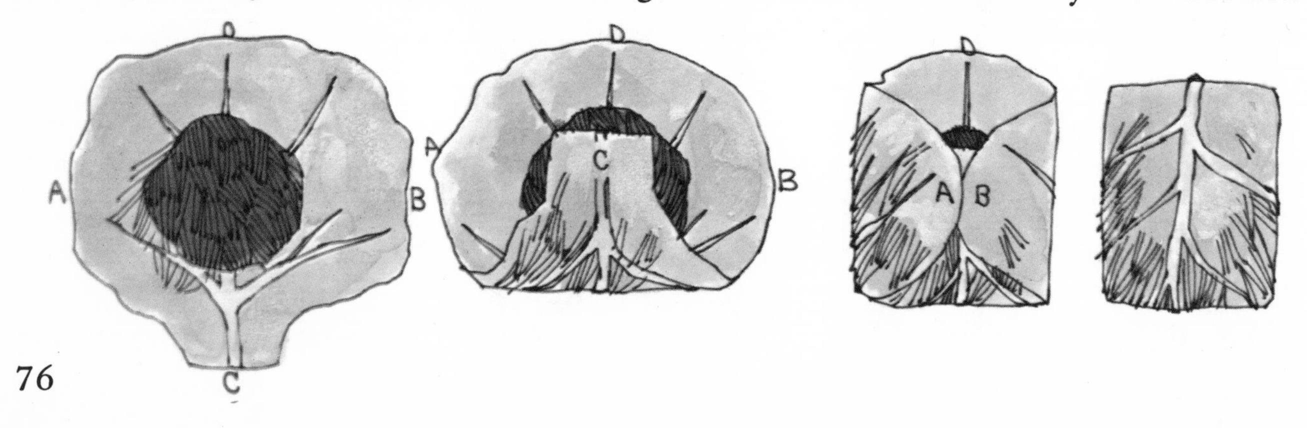

cabbages, seam-side down, in the pot. Mix the remaining ingredients until the sugar dissolves. Carefully cover the top layer of rolls with the whole tomatoes, using your hands to do this. Pour the sauce over the cabbages, making certain that it goes to the bottom of the pot. Bake covered in a 375° oven for 1 hour. Uncover and bake for 2 more hours. Serves 6.

VARIATION: Rinse and drain a large can of sauerkraut. Arrange between the layers of cabbage rolls in the pot before cooking.

MEAT LOAF WITH TOMATO SAUCE

This is a delight when hot with a sauce, cold in a sandwich, or for a late snack.

2 pounds lean ground beef
1 pound ground veal
2 large chopped onions
2 tablespoons chicken fat
1 large peeled, shredded potato
2 large shredded carrots
2 crushed cloves garlic
2 tablespoons minced parsley
1/2 cup uncooked rolled oats
3 large eggs
Salt, pepper, paprika

Mix the ground beef and veal. Saute the onions in the fat until brown. Cool and add to the meat with the remaining ingredients, gently but thoroughly mixing together. If the mixture is too loose, add more oats. If too dry, add 1 egg yolk. (Play this recipe by ear.) Shape the meat into an oval loaf at least 3 inches high. Place in a roaster and bake in a 375° oven for 1 1/2 hours. Serve immediately. To serve cold, drain on paper towels to remove as much fat as possible. Chill. Serves 8 to 10.

TOMATO SAUCE

2 tablespoons fat
1 large chopped onion
1 thinly sliced green pepper
2 crushed cloves garlic
Salt, pepper, fines herbes
1 large can tomato sauce with bits

Saute the onion and green pepper in the fat until soft. Add the garlic, seasoning, and tomato sauce. Simmer for 30 minutes uncovered. Serve with the meat loaf.

THE CORNED BEEF TO KVELL OVER

Buy more than enough meat. It shrinks during the cooking process.

3 pounds corned beef brisket
1 thinly sliced clove garlic
2 medium carrots
1 large onion
Water

Wash the meat thoroughly. Gash the meat in several places with the tip of a sharp knife. Insert a slice of garlic in each gash. Place the meat, carrots, and onion in a 6-quart pot. Cover with cold water. Bring to a boil; pour off the water. Pour fresh hot water into the pot to just cover the meat. Repeat this procedure three more times. The last time let the meat simmer for 2 hours. When a fork can be inserted in the meat and removed easily, the meat is done. To serve hot, remove from the cooking liquid, slice, and serve. To serve cold, let it cool on a platter, wrap well in plastic wrap, and chill. Thinly slice when cold and serve with several mustards, pickles, onion rings, breads, rolls, cole slaw, and baked beans.

THE MAVIN'S WAY TO PICKLE BEEF OR TONGUE

This beats delicatessen corned beef by a mile!

3 pounds beef brisket or beef tongue
1 quart cold water
2 teaspoons pickling spices (minus the red peppers)
5 chopped cloves garlic
4 bay leaves
3 tablespoons salt
1 teaspoon saltpeter

Buy thick brisket well marbled with fat. This is a cheaper cut, usually, but turns out to be more suitable for this recipe. Use the exact recommended weight of meat because the other ingredients are calibrated for this. Be especially careful when measuring saltpeter; use exactly the amount listed. Place the meat in a deep glass bowl or a stoneware crock. Pour the quart of water into another glass bowl.

Add the remaining ingredients, mix together, and pour over the meat; add enough water to cover. Tightly cover and refrigerate. It is best to keep this in the coldest part of the refrigerator. Mark your calendar: For best results, marinate for 19 days. Every 2 days turn the meat, using wooden spoons. Add water if necessary, but ONLY A LITTLE BIT, or the meat might spoil. At the end of the pickling period, discard the pickling water, and wash the meat with cold water. It is ready to cook.

FRESH TONGUE IN TOMATO SAUCE

Here is a perfect dish for a buffet.

3 pounds fresh-cooked beef tongue
1/4 cup chicken fat
2 large onions
4 minced cloves garlic
1 1/2 cups tomato puree
Salt and pepper
1 teaspoon dried fines herbes
1 teaspoon dry hot mustard
1 small can chopped black olives
1/3 cup drained capers
1/3 cup minced parsley

Slice the tongue when it is cold. Saute the onions and garlic until soft and translucent. Add the tomato puree, salt, pepper, fines herbes, and dry mustard. Bring to a slow boil. Remove from the heat. Carefully add the sliced tongue, coating it with the sauce. Replace the skillet on the range. Simmer for 30 minutes. Check it often, and gently turn the meat slices from time to time. Before serving mix the chopped olives and capers into the sauce. Turn into a serving dish. Garnish with chopped parsley. Serves 8.

PICKLED TONGUE

Before you say "Ugh!" - try this recipe.

1 pickled beef tongue (about 3 pounds)
1 large onion
1 bay leaf
4 cloves garlic
1 handful of fresh parsley

Place the tongue in a 6-quart pot, cover with cold water, and bring to a boil. Skim off any scum on the surface and discard. Add the rest of the ingredients, cover the pot, and lower the heat. Simmer for 2 1/2 hours. Test with a fork; do not overcook, for it gets mushy. Allow 50 minutes cooking time per pound. When the tongue is done, remove it from the cooking liquid. Place on paper towels to blot the excess liquid. The tongue will have to be skinned, a very easy task. Using a very sharp knife and your fingers, you will see where the skin is easiest to lift with a little help. It will come off somewhat like a glove. Trim the underpart of the tongue, where there is a great deal of fat. Check the root of the tongue where there are small bones that must be removed. Unless you are going to serve it immediately, cool, wrap in plastic wrap, and refrigerate the meat. It slices best when cold. Use a sharp knife and cut on the diagonal. Start from the root and work toward the tip. This gives larger, better looking slices. Tongue tastes best when served at room temperature. Unless the weather is very hot, remove the meat from the refrigerator about 15 to 20 minutes before serving. Accompany tongue with the same foods as corned beef.

TONGUE IN SWEET AND SOUR SAUCE

3 pounds fresh-cooked beef tongue
1/2 cup seedless raisins
1/2 cup chopped pitted prunes
1 1/2 cups water
1/2 cup unsweetened prune juice
1/4 cup chicken fat
1 chopped green pepper
1 large chopped onion
1/4 cup dark brown sugar
3 tablespoons cornstarch
1/2 cup white vinegar
Salt and pepper

Place the washed raisins and prunes in a saucepan. Pour the water and prune juice over them. Bring to a boil, cover, reduce the heat and simmer for 30 minutes.

Saute the onions and green pepper until soft. Mix the brown sugar and cornstarch. Add to the onion mixture with the vinegar, raisins, and prunes. Cook over medium heat stirring constantly until the sauce thickens and boils. Cook another 5 minutes to eliminate the cornstarch taste. Taste and adjust the seasoning. Add the tongue slices and heat gently for 30 minutes. Serves 8.

SAUERKRAUT GULYAS

2 pounds sauerkraut
1/4 cup chicken fat
3 large chopped onions
4 minced cloves garlic
3 tablespoons sweet Hungarian paprika
2 tablespoons caraway seeds
2 pounds veal in 1 1/2 inch cubes
1 1/2 cups drained canned tomatoes
Salt and pepper
1 1/3 cups chicken stock
2 tablespoons granulated flour
2/3 cup tomato puree
1 teaspoon dried dill

Rinse the sauerkraut with cold water to eliminate the briny taste. Saute the onions and garlic in fat until tender, using a 6-quart pot. Add the paprika and caraway seeds, mixing well. Add the veal and saute gently on all sides. Add the tomatoes and season with salt and pepper. Add the sauerkraut and 1 cup of chicken stock. Simmer or bake in a 325° oven for 1 1/2 hours until tender. Whisk the flour into 1/3 cup stock. Then add the puree, whisking until smooth. Add this to the meat mixture and cook for 10 more minutes. Garnish with dill. Serves 6.

HUNGARIAN GULYAS

Galuska and cucumber salad are the classic accompaniments for this entree.

3 large chopped onions
1 1/2 pounds chuck in 1 1/2-inch cubes
1/2 pound veal in 1 1/2-inch cubes
1 thinly sliced green pepper
1 large peeled, seeded, diced tomato
1 tablespoon tomato paste
1/4 cup chicken fat
1 tablespoon sweet Hungarian paprika
Salt

Saute the onions in fat in a 5-quart pot until golden brown. Add the meat and paprika. Cover, and simmer for 10 minutes. Stir at least twice, adding a little water if needed. Add the green pepper, diced tomato, tomato paste, and 1 teaspoon salt. Mix thoroughly, adding 1 1/2 cups water. Cover and simmer or bake in a 300° oven for 2 hours until the meat is tender. Stir occasionally, adding water only if necessary. This dish should not be soupy. Adjust the seasoning before serving. Serves 5.

STUFFED BREAST OF VEAL

When I was a child this was the star attraction of special dinners. At the time I thought the stuffing the rare delight. Later, when I had tasted restaurant food and tried to cook, I appreciated the veal. The kosher restaurant, Blooms, in London, is the only place where I can say that it resembled Grandma's cooking. The veal should be tender and juicy with the bones and cartilage almost falling apart. The meat shrinks so buy more than enough. To run out of food is the worst sin in the balaboosta's kitchen!

1 1/2 tablespoons chicken fat
1/2 cup water
1 1/2 large diced onions
3 chopped garlic cloves
5 1/2 pound breast of veal with
a pocket for stuffing

Place the fat and water in the bottom of a roaster large enough to accommodate the meat. Stuff the pocket with stuffing and sew it shut with a darning needle and thread. Place the meat on a rack in the roaster with the ribs on the bottom. Place

SILVERSMITHS AT WORK

the covered roaster in a 425° oven until the meat sizzles. Reduce the heat to 400° for about 45 minutes. Finally reduce the oven temperature to 375°. Total cooking time should be about 3 hours. Baste frequently to prevent the veal from drying out. If the roaster cover is not a tight fit, cover it tightly with aluminum foil.

Meat Stuffing:
- 1/2 pound baby-beef liver
- 2 tablespoons chicken fat
- 1 medium diced onion
- 1/2 cup diced celery
- 1/4 cup diced green pepper
- 1 large egg
- Salt, pepper, paprika, poultry seasoning
- 2 large minced cloves garlic
- 1 1/2-inch-thick slice firm white bread, crust removed
- 1/2 pound peeled, cooked, quartered chestnuts

Cut the liver into several pieces. Place in a saucepan and cover with cold water. Bring just to a boil; remove from the heat, drain, and cool. Saute the onion, celery, and green pepper in fat until the onions are golden. Remove from the heat and cool. Combine the onion mixture with the egg, seasoning, and garlic. Soak the bread in water; gently squeeze out the liquid and add the bread to the onions. Combine with the liver and put the entire mixture through the medium blade of a food grinder. Add the chestnuts; the stuffing is now ready to use. If you would like to bake the stuffing, grease a casserole, place the stuffing in it, cover, and bake in a 350° oven for 1 hour. Uncover during the last 15 minutes for a crusty top.

CHOPPED LUNG

This dish has a rich, savory gravy. Try it with rice or potatoes.

1 beef lung
1/2 teaspoon salt
1 large chopped onion
3 minced cloves garlic
1/2 chopped green pepper
1 chopped stalk celery
1 can (8-ounce) tomato sauce
Salt, pepper, paprika, poultry seasoning

Sauce:
1 tablespoon chicken fat
1/2 small minced onion
1 tablespoon granulated flour
Lung gravy

Wash the lung thoroughly. Cut into 2-inch cubes. Cover the lung with water in an 8-quart pot, adding 1/2 teaspoon salt. Bring to a boil. Cook over medium heat, half covered, for an hour, making certain there is always enough water in the pot to cover the meat. When the meat is cooked, drain, discard the cooking liquid, and cool the meat. Put the meat through the coarse blade of the meat grinder. Place the chopped onion, garlic, green pepper, and celery in a 6-quart pot or a large skillet. Add the lung and the remaining ingredients. Stir, bringing to a slow boil over medium heat. Reduce the heat and simmer for 1 hour. Make a roux. Saute the minced onion in fat until soft. Add the flour and whisk constantly. The mixture should get a rich, golden appearance. Slowly add some of the gravy from the lung mixture, stirring constantly. Keep adding some of the gravy, stirring, until thickened and smooth. Add this sauce to the original lung mixture. Simmer for another 30 minutes. Taste and reseason. Serves 6 to 8.

BRUST

Jewish cooks serve brust for company. Buy enough to allow for second helpings!

4 1/2 pounds boneless brisket
3 sliced cloves garlic
Salt, pepper, paprika
1 cup water
3 chopped garlic cloves
1 large chopped onion
1 large peeled, seeded, diced tomato

Make deep thin gashes in the meat and insert slivers of garlic. Season with salt, pepper, and paprika on all sides. Generously grease a roasting pan; place the meat in it. Place the roaster in a 500° oven, turning the meat to brown evenly on all sides. When the meat is brown remove the roaster from the oven. Add the remaining ingredients. Reduce the oven temperature to 325°. Cover the roaster and cook in the oven for about 2 hours, turning every 30 minutes. Test with a fork to be sure it is done. Delicious hot or cold.

MILTZ

2 beef miltz (spleen)
2 teaspoons salt
Pepper, paprika, poultry seasoning
1 large chopped onion
1 can (8-ounce) tomato sauce
1 chopped stalk celery
3 minced cloves garlic
1 thinly sliced green pepper
Water to cover
6 peeled and quartered potatoes

Have the butcher remove the skin from both sides of the miltz. Cut the miltz into 1 1/2 inch thick slices, and place them in an 8-quart pot. Add the remaining ingredients except the potatoes. Bring to a slow boil over medium heat. Reduce the heat and simmer, watching carefully because miltz can stick to the pan. After 1 1/2 hours, add the potatoes, and cook for 30 minutes. Stir throughout the cooking period, adding water if needed. Serves 6 to 8.

STUFFED HELZEL

Would you believe stuffed chicken-neck skins? Delicious!

8 large chicken-neck skins

Stuffing:
- 1 pound lean ground beef
- 1/2 small grated onion
- 2 crushed cloves garlic
- 1 large egg
- Salt, pepper, paprika, poultry seasoning
- 1/2 cup raw rice

Gravy:
- 1 can (8-ounce) tomato sauce with bits
- 1/2 green pepper
- Bay leaf
- 1 1/2 cups water
- 1 whole onion
- 1 stalk celery
- Salt, pepper, paprika, poultry seasoning

Salt the helzels; wash in cold water. Mix all the stuffing ingredients thoroughly.

Sew together an end of each helzel before stuffing, using a darning needle and doubled white thread. Stuff the helzels; sew each open end together. Do not pack the stuffing in tightly because the rice must expand. Put the remaining ingredients in the bottom of a roasting pan. Lay the stuffed helzels on top of this. Cover the pan; place in a 375° oven. Bake for 1 hour. Turn the helzels frequently, basting them. Uncover the pan 15 to 20 minutes before they are done. Watch closely for overbrowning. Slice before serving. Helzels are good hot or cold. Remember to remove the string before serving. Allow at least 1 helzel per person.

STUFFED DERMA

3 feet narrow beef casings or 6 large helzels (chicken-neck skins)
3/4 cup + 2 tablespoons granulated flour
4 tablespoons farina
1 1/2 teaspoons paprika
Salt
Freshly ground pepper
1/2 cup + 1 tablespoon chicken fat
2 tablespoons grieben
1/2 small grated onion
3 crushed cloves garlic

Remove all fat from the casings, being careful not to tear them. Turn them inside out; clean thoroughly. Mix all the other ingredients well. Sew up one end of the casing; fill it lightly. (You stuff the casings inside-out.) Sew the end of the casing using the doubled white thread and a darning needle. Tie off the casing tightly at 1-foot intervals, like a tourniquet. You will have a long string of individually tied derma. Bring 8 quarts of water to a boil. Place the derma in this water. Simmer for 45 minutes. Drain, and discard any fat on the casing. Cool and freeze, or continue, using the following ingredients.

1/4 cup melted chicken fat
2 large peeled and sliced onions
2 cloves garlic
1 cup drained canned tomatoes

Arrange the ingredients in a roaster in an even layer. Use a sharp, pointed needle to prick the derma all over, allowing excess fat to escape. Bake, uncovered, in a 350° oven for 1 hour, basting frequently, until brown. Cut the derma apart at the cord and slice. Serve hot with a meat meal. Yield: 6 portions.

LAMB SEPHARDIT

The distinctive Arabic seasoning in this dish is found in the foods of the Jews from North Africa. Rice pilaf is especially appropriate with this lamb dish.

3 tablespoons chicken fat
2 pounds lean lamb cut into 1-inch cubes
3 large chopped onions
3 minced cloves garlic
6 peeled, seeded, chopped tomatoes
1 cup beef stock
2 pounds fresh green beans, in 2-inch lengths
Salt and pepper
1/8 teaspoon cinnamon
A pinch of each of the following:
White pepper, ground nutmeg, ground cloves, ground cardamom

Saute the lamb cubes in fat, browning them evenly on all sides in a 5-quart pot. Add the onions and garlic. Continue sauteing until they are golden brown. Add the diced tomatoes and the stock. Cover the pot, reduce the heat, and simmer for 1 hour or place the pot in a 325° oven for the hour. Add the green beans and the seasonings, adjusting to your taste. Simmer either on top of the range or in the oven for 30 minutes until the beans and meat are tender. Serves 6.

AUNT ROSIE'S CHOLENT

How well I remember when visiting my aunt and uncle, being served this specialty of the house and urged to eat until there seemed no stopping. In Europe the mother took the cholent to a community oven (usually the baker's), on Friday morning. One of the children picked it up after services on Shabbat (Saturday noon) for the midday meal. Thus the most observant Jewish family could have a hot meal on the Sabbath without contravening the laws.

1/3 cup chicken fat
4 large chopped onions
4 pounds beef flanken
1 1/2 cups dried lima beans
3/4 cup pearl barley (coarse)
6 large carrots, halved lengthwide, cut into 3-inch strips
Salt and pepper
3 teaspoons paprika
4 minced cloves garlic
Boiling water to cover

Saute the onions in fat until golden. Add the beef and cook it until both the meat and onions are well browned. Place them in a large pot with a tight-fitting lid. Add the remaining ingredients. Cover tightly and place in a 250° oven for 24 hours. The long, slow cooking blends the flavors for a delectable dish. Serves 8.

VARIATION: If you can buy smoked goose, place a leg and half of the breast in the cholent after the meat and onions have been browned. This gives an indescribably delicious flavor to the cholent.

ESSIG FLEISCH

This dunker's delight is served in a shallow bowl with plenty of rye bread.

2 tablespoons chicken fat
5 pounds lean boneless chuck
Salt and pepper
5 thinly sliced onions
5 minced cloves garlic
Fines herbes
3/4 cup apple juice
1 1/2 cups tomato sauce with bits
1 tablespoon honey
Lemon juice to taste

Cut the meat in 3-inch cubes, trimming off all the fat or gristle. Saute the meat in the fat until well browned on all sides in a 6-quart pot. This seals the juices in the meat. Season the meat as it is browning. When it is done, remove to a platter. Reduce the heat; add the onions and garlic. Simmer until soft, seasoning with more salt and pepper. Return the meat to the pot, adding fines herbes and apple juice. Cover and simmer until tender, about 2 to 3 hours, or bake in a 325° oven. Turn the meat from time to time. Add the tomato sauce and honey when the meat is done. Taste and adjust the seasoning. Serves 8 to 10.

GEDEMPTE FLEISCH WITH APRICOTS

This combination of meat and fruit in a sweet-sour sauce is typically Jewish.

2 tablespoons chicken fat
3 pounds lean boneless chuck
Salt and pepper
5 large thinly sliced onions
5 minced cloves garlic
Fines herbes
Cinnamon
1/2 cup moist-pack dried apricots
2 pounds chicken legs
Paprika
6 large carrots, halved lengthwise and cut into 3-inch strips
Lemon juice
Brown sugar (twice the amount of lemon juice)

Cut the chuck in 6 pieces, trimming away fat. Saute a few pieces of meat at a time in hot fat in a 6-quart pot. Season the meat as it browns on all sides. Remove the meat to a platter. Brown the remaining meat. After it is removed from the pot reduce the heat; add the onions and garlic. Cook until soft but not brown, seasoning with salt and pepper. Add fines herbes and cinnamon. Replace the meat in the pot. Cover and simmer for 1 1/2 hours or bake in a 325° oven. Turn the meat from time to time.

Remove the meat to a platter. Place the chicken legs in the pot, seasoning with salt, pepper, paprika, and cinnamon. Add the apricots, placing the meat back in the pot on top of them. Cook until the chicken is tender, turning from time to time to evenly brown the chicken. Be careful to keep the apricots from the bottom of the pan. Cook about 1 hour. Add water only if the dish is in danger of burning. Add the carrots 30 minutes before serving. Place them in the bottom of the pot so they cook in the pan juices. Taste and correct the seasoning, adding lemon juice and brown sugar to taste. Generously serves 6 to 8.

TURKEY THE WAY A YIDDISH MAMA MAKES IT

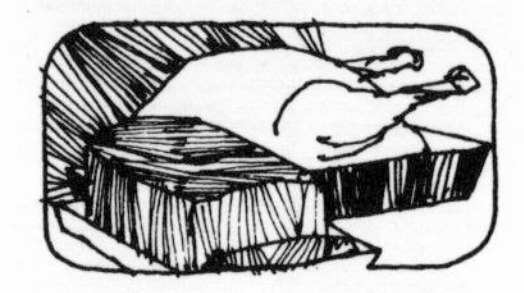

The biggest complaint I always have when I order turkey in a restaurant is its total lack of seasoning. As you have gathered from the other recipes in this book, Jewish cooking depends heavily on onion, garlic, and seasonings for its tam – that incredible taste sensation created by the subtle blending of flavors. Make it like Mama does!

1 turkey (about 13 pounds)
Chicken fat
6 crushed cloves garlic
1 large onion
2 chopped celery stalks and leaves
4 sprigs parsley
3 cloves garlic
Kosher salt
3 chopped onions
1/4 cup chopped celery tops
4 cloves garlic
1 turkey neck
1/4 cup beef or chicken stock
8 peppercorns

Place the turkey on a large piece of foil. Rub the entire surface with softened chicken fat and crushed garlic. Place the whole onion, celery, parsley, and garlic in the turkey cavities (the large and small one). Generously grease the bottom of the roasting pan with chicken fat. Arrange the chopped onions in an even layer in the bottom of the roaster. Truss the bird, using a trussing needle and thin white cord, making sure the legs are tied together and the wings kept close to the body, and the cavities are sewn shut. Place the turkey in the roasting pan on the bed of onions. Season on all sides with kosher salt. Roast uncovered in a 450° oven for 20 minutes.

Remove from the oven. Add the remaining ingredients to the roasting pan. Reduce the oven temperature to 350°. Cover the roaster and continue cooking until the bird is done, basting every 20 to 30 minutes. Make certain there is always just enough liquid to cover the bottom of the pan. When you begin to have too much liquid and it starts to touch the bottom of the turkey, remove some of the liquid with a baster. Return these pan juices to the roaster when the turkey is done. The turkey should roast a total of about 4 hours. Check to see if the leg moves easily. The last 30 minutes you can uncover the bird for a crisp brown skin. Turn the bird from side to side during the roasting if you prefer. I leave mine sitting on its back.

Let the bird sit in the pan for 20 to 30 minutes before carving. Remove the cord. A turkey is easier to carve when cold. It can be served cold or gently reheated later, well wrapped in foil, at a temperature of 325°. Or serve it hot immediately after carving it. Unless you have a talented husband or a gift for surgery yourself, make your mistakes in the kitchen. They will not show when you serve the meat on the platter.

Remove the fat from the pan juices in the bottom of the roaster. Add any reserved excess juices. If you want to thicken these juices remove the bird, bring the juices to a boil and reduce the volume of the liquid by half. Mash the vegetables with a wooden spoon. You can sprinkle 2 tablespoons granulated flour over it while stirring. Cook at least 5 minutes.

Matzo Stuffing: If you wish to use stuffing, be sure to allow extra cooking time.

3/4 cup chicken fat
3 large chopped onions
1 cup minced celery
1/2 pound chopped mushrooms
1 cup chopped walnuts
1 cooked chopped turkey giblet
2 large tart chopped apples
10 finely crushed matzos
Salt, pepper, paprika
1 large egg + 1 egg yolk
2 cans undiluted kosher chicken soup

Saute the onions, celery, and mushrooms in fat until golden. Add the nuts, giblet, and matzos; toss well. Remove from heat, and add remaining ingredients.

CRUSADER WALL
- ACRE

Fish

Observant Jews are restricted in their choice of fish, which must have fins and scales. This excludes all shellfish, for example. Most of the traditional cooking is European featuring fresh-water fish, such as pike, carp, and whitefish. When I traveled in Israel I saw the pools where the carp are raised. It is the favorite ingredient of gefilte fish, the most popular fish dish in any Jewish cook's repertoire.

The three recipes in this section are my favorites. Boiled Pike, served cold, is the equal of the fanciest chaudfroid. Baked Fish, which features shad, is second to no other with its delicate, subtle flavor. Sweet and Sour Fish shows the versatility of the fish and its treatment. This is also best served cold, good in both summer and winter.

Within the limits of religious law Jewish cooks have exercised their ingenuity to produce these deliciously different gourmet recipes.

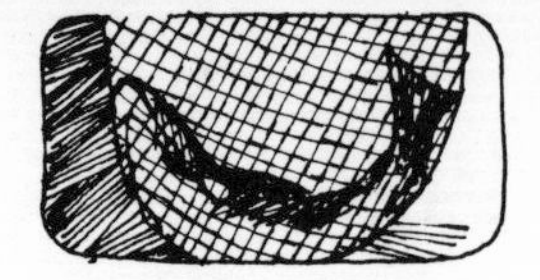

BOILED PIKE

2 pike heads, cleaned by the fish vendor
1 large quartered onion
1 peeled, seeded, quartered tomato
3 sprigs parsley
Salt, pepper, paprika
3 1/2 pounds yellow pike
2 medium quartered potatoes
1/2 tablespoon white vinegar

Cover the fish heads, onion, tomato, parsley, celery, and seasoning with water in a 6-quart pot. Bring to a slow boil uncovered; reduce the heat and simmer for 20 minutes. Cut the pike into 3-inch-thick chunks. Carefully place them in the broth. Add the remaining ingredients, simmering gently until the fish flakes easily, about 25 to 30 minutes. Remove the heads from the broth. Serve hot or cold. The broth jells like an aspic when chilled. Serves 6.

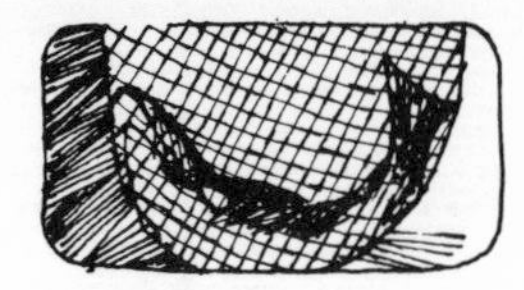

BAKED FISH

When you bake shad, many of the tiny bones soften, making it a joy to eat.

1 large sliced onion
3 pounds shad or yellow pike
Salt, pepper, paprika

Grease a shallow baking pan generously with shortening. Arrange the onion slices in an even layer in the bottom of the pan. Lay the fish on the onions. Season and bake uncovered in a 350° oven for 1 1/2 hours. Serves 6.

SWEET AND SOUR FISH

Sweet and sour entrees are favorites of both Jewish and Pennsylvania-Dutch cooks. This is best when served cold.

1 cleaned carp (about 4 pounds)
Cider vinegar
2 large thinly sliced onions
Pepper
2 thinly sliced lemons
1/3 cup raisins
6 gingersnaps
Brown sugar

Place the fish in a bowl. Cover it with cider vinegar and let stand covered overnight. (This considerably firms the fish, preventing its falling apart while cooking.) Drain the fish the next day. Place it in the cooking pot. Measure the amount of water needed to just cover it. Remove the fish, draining it on paper towels. Add the onions to the water and bring just to a boil. Replace the fish in the pot, reducing the heat, and simmer gently for 1 3/4 hours. After 1 hour, add the pepper, lemon slices and raisins. When the fish is done, remove to a platter.

Add the crumbled gingersnaps to the sauce as a thickening agent. Add more for a thicker sauce. Correct the sweet-sour balance by adding brown sugar. For additional tartness add some cider vinegar. Serves 6.

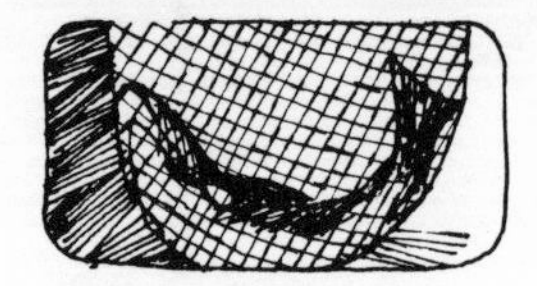

GIVETCH

This Roumanian vegetable stew with fish is a perfect hot dish for a buffet.

3 large peeled potatoes, sliced crosswise 1/4 inches thick
3 large sliced onions, separated into rings
2 green peppers, thinly sliced lengthwise
3 pounds fresh peas OR 2 packages frozen peas
1 pound fresh green beans OR 1 package frozen green beans
1 pound fresh sliced mushrooms
2 packages frozen lima beans
2 fresh peeled, quartered tomatoes
1/2 cup olive oil
1/4 cup water
Salt, pepper, paprika, crushed garlic, fines herbes to taste
1 large (about 4 pounds) piece salmon, carp, or whitefish

Line the bottom of a casserole with a single layer of sliced potatoes. Stand sliced potatoes around the four sides of the casserole. Thaw frozen vegetables, patting dry on paper towels before using. Season the potato layer and add single layers of the onions, green pepper, peas, green beans, mushrooms, and lima beans, seasoning each layer.

Place the tomatoes in each corner of the dish. The remaining sliced potatoes are the top layer of vegetables. Brush the potatoes with oil, place the fish in the center of the dish, seasoning it well. Brush with oil. Pour the remaining oil evenly in the four corners of the dish. Add the water to the dish in the same way. Bake in a preheated 325° oven for 2 hours, or until tender and done. Serves 8 graciously.

CITY
COPPER ARTS
JERUSALEM

Pastries and Breads

The bread and coffeecakes included in this section are staples in the Jewish cuisine. Many people finish each meal, no matter how elaborate, by having a slice of bread. Jews are extremely conscious of bread; they include it in most religious ceremonies with a blessing, and serve a variety of breads and rolls with meals. Kuchen, a yeast coffeecake, is served with breakfast, lunch, and between-meal snacks. Wherever we traveled in Israel, traditional Jewish hospitality was extended, often by complete strangers. We were always served coffee and cake, frequently kuchen. It is even served when stale as a dunker.

No meal is complete in a Jewish home without a little dessert, little being a meaningless word. It usually means fruit and cake or cookies. There are too many for me to include here so I chose my own favorites. No Jewish cookbook could be written without sponge cake, cheesecake, and hamantaschen. I hope that you will enjoy serving these pastries to your family and friends.

KUCHEN

The Hotel Reich in Jerusalem serves this distinctive kuchen for Shabbat breakfast.

Dough:
- 2 packages dry yeast
- 1 teaspoon sugar
- 1/4 cup lukewarm water
- 1/2 cup evaporated milk
- 1/2 cup sweet butter
- 3 1/2 cups sifted all-purpose flour
- 1/2 cup sugar
- 1 teaspoon salt
- 3 large eggs
- 1/2 cup sour cream
- 1 teaspoon vanilla

Add dry yeast and 1 teaspoon sugar to the lukewarm water. Be sure all the yeast and sugar are completely dissolved. Heat the milk and sweet butter over low heat just until the butter has melted. Remove from the heat; cool to room temperature. Mix 2 cups flour, 1/2 cup sugar, and 1 teaspoon salt in a large mixing bowl. Pour in the cooled milk, add the yeast, and mix thoroughly. Next add the rest of the ingredients except for the remaining 1 1/2 cups flour and mix thoroughly. Finally add the 1 1/2 cups flour, beating until smooth for at least 5 minutes. Cover the bowl with a linen cloth; place in a warm draft-free place to double in size. Beat vigorously, cover, and let it rise again. Beat it again just for a little while, making certain to mix all of the dough. Cover the bowl with plastic wrap; chill overnight in the refrigerator.

Generously butter a 10-inch tube pan the next day. Place the dough on a lightly floured pastry board. Gently coat it on all sides with flour. Do not knead the flour into the dough. Roll the dough into a 1/2-inch-thick circle about 16 inches in diameter. Spread the filling evenly on the dough, rolling it up like a jelly roll. The rolled circle will naturally overlap in the pan, giving a better shape. Place the roll in the tube pan, arranging it so the ends of the roll overlap. Cover with the linen cloth; let it rise again in a warm place. When it is ready the dough should almost reach the top of the pan. Uncover, brush the top of the kuchen with milk, and bake in a 325° oven for 1 hour. Let the cake cool in the pan before removing.

This freezes beautifully and should be reheated before serving. There is nothing that can compete with the taste of freshly baked kuchen. Serve with butter and jam. Slice 1/3 inch or more thick. If stale, toast the kuchen.

Filling:
- 1 can poppyseed filling (Solo)
- 2 ounces grated sweet chocolate
- Grated rind of 1 orange
- 1/4 cup dried currants, plumped by steaming them over boiling water

Mix all the ingredients together.

Raisin-Nut Filling:
- 1/3 cup plumped raisins
- 1/3 cup chopped pecans
- Cinnamon
- 1/3 cup brown sugar
- 3 tablespoons softened butter

Combine the raisins, nuts, cinnamon and sugar. Spread the butter over the dough before sprinkling it with the filling.

VARIATION: The above filling can be combined with fruit. Spread the dough with 1/3 cup strawberry preserves instead of the butter before sprinkling on the rest of the ingredients.

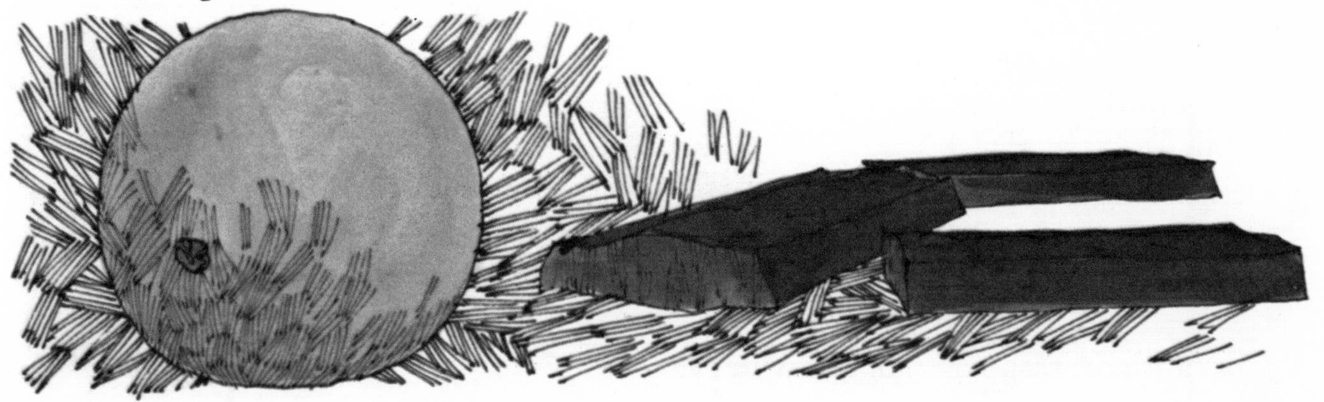

RUGELACH

Make these when you want a little something special.

1 package dry yeast
2 tablespoons sugar
1/4 cup lukewarm water
1 can (5 ounce) evaporated milk
3 egg yolks
1 teaspoon vanilla
3 cups unsifted flour
1/2 teaspoon salt
1 cup softened butter
1/2 cup sugar
2 1/2 tablespoons cinnamon
1/3 cup finely chopped nuts
Jam (apricot, raspberry, or strawberry)

Dissolve the yeast and 2 tablespoons sugar in the water. Beat the egg yolks, evaporated milk, and vanilla with a whisk. Mix the flour and salt together, adding the butter, egg mixture, and yeast to the mixing bowl. Use an electric mixer to beat until mixture is blended and smooth. Tightly cover bowl with plastic wrap. Refrigerate overnight. Mix the 1/2 cup sugar and cinnamon together. Sprinkle the pastry board with some of the cinnamon sugar. Divide the dough into 6 parts. Roll each into a circle 6 inches in diameter. Use a sharp knife to cut the circle into 8 wedges. Place 1/2 teaspoon jam and some nuts on the widest part of each wedge. Roll the pastries from the wide part to the point. Place them on a parchment-paper-lined cooky sheet with the pastry resting on the seam, curving each one slightly into a crescent. Bake in a 350° oven for 30 minutes until golden brown. Makes 4 dozen. These freeze beautifully but I love them warm and fresh from the oven. Reheat them wrapped in foil when you serve them after they have been frozen.

CHALLAH

Challah is the traditional bread served at the Sabbath meal and all festive and religious ceremonies, except Passover and fast days. Cooks are known for their intricate artistic loaves. Cutting and serving the bread has a prescribed ritual for the devout Jew much like the Japanese tea ceremony. This recipe is unique because it does not contain eggs.

1 1/2 packages dry yeast
1 tablespoon sugar
1/2 cup lukewarm water
4 cups all-purpose flour
1 cup lukewarm water
1 tablespoon sugar
1 1/2 teaspoons salt
2 tablespoons homogenized shortening

Place the yeast and 1 tablespoon sugar in a bowl. Add 1/2 cup lukewarm water, mixing well. The yeast should dissolve and start to bubble. Measure the flour into a large bowl. Pour the bubbling yeast into a well made in the center of the flour. Add the remaining ingredients; knead the dough. Stand the mixing bowl on a damp cloth to anchor it. Knead the dough with the heel of your hand. Be sure to get all the dough away from the sides and bottom of the bowl. Keep kneading until the dough begins to blister and comes off your hands. Lightly coat the surface of the dough with the shortening. Cover the bowl with a clean linen towel. Set it in a warm place to raise for about 40 minutes. After 40 minutes, test the dough by plunging your finger into the center of the mound of dough. If your indentation remains in then it has raised sufficiently. Divide the dough into 4 parts. Pat and roll each of the 3 parts into a long cylinder and braid the three cylinders together. Divide the remaining part into 3 small parts, form into cylinders, and braid. Place the small braid on top of the large one. Place it on a greased baking sheet. Cover again with the towel. Raise in a warm place until the dough is almost doubled. This takes 30 to 40 minutes. Place the challah in a 400° oven on a greased baking sheet. Immediately reduce the temperature to 375° baking for 50 minutes. The bread should be well browned and crusty. Cool on a rack.

NOTE: Brush the surface of the challah with a mixture of 1 egg yolk and 2 tablespoons water, and sprinkle with poppyseeds just before baking, for a special crust.

HAMANTASCHEN

Hamantaschen are a traditional food during Purim. This festival dating from the Book of Esther is a celebration of the triumph of righteousness and perhaps a little women's lib, also. There are many versions of hamantaschen, all having the same inimitable shape – a triangular pastry with the sides all meeting over the filling. This is supposed to be in memory of the wicked villain – Haman and his hat. Sometimes I shape mine so a little of the filling peeks through. That way my family can identify them – prune or lekvar, poppyseed (mohn) or cheese.

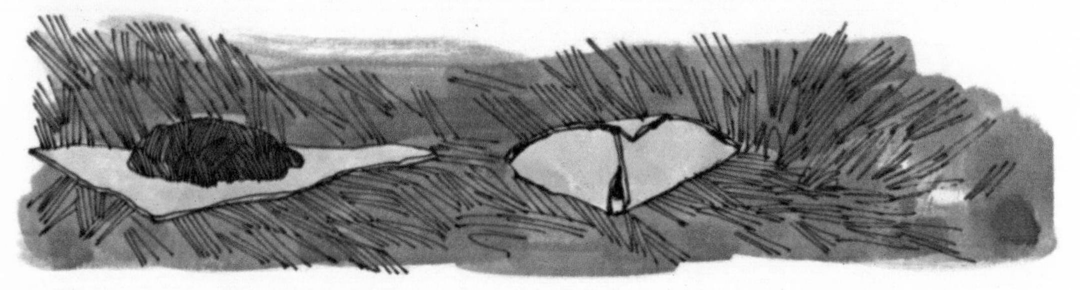

Dough: 4 cups flour
1 teaspoon salt
1 cup homogenized shortening
1 package dry yeast
1/4 cup warm water
1 large egg + 2 egg yolks
1 cup sour cream
1 teaspoon vanilla
Grated rind of 1 lemon
2/3 cup sugar

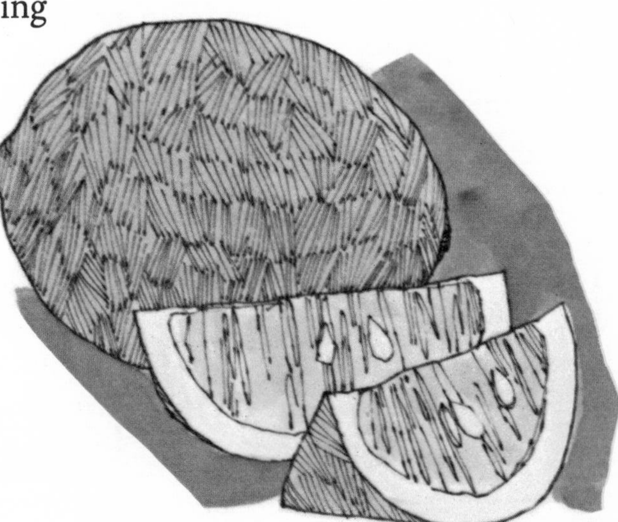

Glaze: 1 large egg
1 tablespoon water
1 teaspoon sugar
1 teaspoon oil

Sift the flour and salt into a large bowl. Cut the shortening into the flour mixture until the lumps are the size of small peas. Dissolve the yeast in water. Use a whisk to beat the egg yolks, sour cream, yeast, vanilla, and lemon rind together until smooth. Add this to the flour, kneading with your hands until it is thoroughly mixed, the dough coming away from the sides of the bowl. Cover the bowl tightly with plastic wrap; refrigerate for 2 hours. The timing is very important with this dough. The consistency changes if you keep it refrigerated too long.

Sprinkle some sugar on the pastry board. Divide the dough into 2 parts. Keep one refrigerated while you are rolling out the other. Place the dough on the sugared board, and sprinkle with sugar. Roll to a 12-inch square or circle. Fold one side and then the other toward the center, making 3 layers of dough. Repeat the procedure after giving the dough a quarter turn. Remember to sprinkle more sugar on the board and the dough. This dough should then be rolled as thin as possible or about 1/4-inch thick. The dough will rise as you are working with it.

Cut the dough into 3-inch circles; place a teaspoon of filling in the center of each. Bring all the edges to the middle, pinching them shut but leaving a small opening in the center where the filling can be seen. Place on a teflon cooky sheet.

Mix the glaze ingredients together, being sure to dissolve the sugar. Brush the hamantaschen with the glaze; bake in a 375° oven for 22 to 25 minutes until golden brown. Yield: about 4 dozen, depending how thin you have rolled the dough. These freeze beautifully. Be sure to reheat them in foil before serving.

continued

Prune Filling:

I purchase prune filling. The imported versions are made from the Svetchen plum not found in this country. It is sold either as Lekvar or Powidl depending on whether it comes from Hungary or Germany. Use it straight from the jar; it is perfect. Do not use the American version; it tastes like glue.

Poppyseed Filling:

- 2 cups ground poppyseed
- 2 cups milk
- 1 cup plumped raisins
- 1/4 cup chopped almonds
- 1/4 cup butter
- 1/4 cup light corn syrup
- 1 teaspoon vanilla

Place all the ingredients except the vanilla in a saucepan. Bring to a boil, stirring; simmer over medium heat until the mixture is thick and the milk absorbed. Cool; add the vanilla.

Cheese Filling: Use the same Rich Dessert Filling recipe given on page 45.

HONEY CAKE

Honey Cake is an integral part of celebrations in Jewish homes and synagogues. At a Brith, Bar Mitzvah, wedding, and on Rosh Hashanah, honey cake assumes its traditional role. We always had it with schnapps.

3 cups all-purpose flour
1 tablespoon cinnamon
1 tablespoon baking soda
1 teaspoon baking powder
1/2 cup homogenized shortening
1 cup sugar
3 large eggs
3/4 cup honey (not whipped)
1 cup triple-strength coffee
1/4 cup chocolate chips
1/4 cup plumped raisins
Grated rind of 1 orange

Sift together the first 4 ingredients. Beat the shortening and sugar together until light and fluffy. Add the eggs, one at a time, alternately with the honey. Add the sifted dry ingredients alternately with the coffee, beginning and ending with the flour. Do not overbeat. Fold the chocolate chips, raisins, and orange rind into the batter. Turn the batter into a greased 10-inch tube pan. Bake in a 325° oven for 1 hour until the cake tests done with a toothpick. Cool it about 30 minutes on a rack. Remove the cake from the pan to complete cooling. Honey cake stays moist and is an excellent dunker when stale.

CHEESECAKE TO SERVE THE MISHPOCHEH

Crust:
- 2 cups sifted flour
- Grated rind of 1 lemon
- 1/2 cup sugar
- 3/4 cup butter
- 2 large egg yolks

Mix the flour, sugar, and lemon rind. Cut the butter into the flour mixture until the crumbs resemble small peas. Add the egg yolks; knead the dough with your hands until it is smooth and holds together. Grease and flour a 10-inch-square metal baking pan. Press the dough into the bottom and sides of the pan, making an even crust.

Filling: 2 cups cottage cheese
1/4 teaspoon salt
1/4 cup granulated flour
4 large eggs
1 cup sugar
1 cup evaporated milk(undiluted)
1 1/2 teaspoons vanilla

Sieve the cottage cheese. Mix it well with the flour. Beat the eggs and salt in an electric mixer until frothy. Add the sugar gradually, beating until the mixture is thick and lighter in color, about 10 minutes. Add the cheese, evaporated milk, and vanilla, mixing until well blended. Pour this into the dough-lined pan. Bake in a 325° oven for 1 hour. Turn off the oven, leaving the cheesecake inside for another hour. Remove from the oven, cool, and refrigerate. Good to serve at room temperature or chilled. Serves 10 to 12.

SPONGE CAKE

This is a favorite feather-light dessert. It can be served plain or frosted.

6 large eggs, separated
Grated rind of 1 orange
1 1/2 cups sugar
1 1/2 cups sifted cake flour
1 1/2 teaspoons baking powder
1/4 teaspoon salt
1/2 cup orange juice

Grease the tube of a 10-inch tube pan. Line the bottom of the pan with waxed paper. Beat the egg yolks well; add the orange rind and sugar. Beat with an electric mixer until the mixture is light and thickened. Add the flour alternately with the orange juice to the yolk mixture, beginning and ending with the flour. Whip the egg whites with the baking powder and salt until the whites stand in stiff peaks. Gently fold the whites into the yolks. Bake in a 325° oven for 1 hour. To cool, hang the cake pan upside down on the neck of a soda bottle. Let the cake stand inverted until the pan is thoroughly cool to the touch (at least several hours). Use a spatula or sharp knife to loosen the cake from the sides of the pan and tube. Remove the cake from the pan. Sponge cake should be served as soon as possible. Be sure to store in a plastic bag to keep fresh. Use either a cake breaker especially designed for sponge and angel cakes, or a very sharp knife when you cut the cake.

MOHN TORTE

1 cup homogenized shortening
1 1/2 cups sugar
1 can (12 ounce) poppyseed filling
2 ounces grated sweet chocolate
Grated rind of 1 orange
1/4 cup apricot jam
4 large eggs, separated
1 teaspoon vanilla
1 cup sour cream
2 1/2 cups sifted all-purpose flour
1 teaspoon baking soda
1 teaspoon salt
1 teaspoon cinnamon

Grease the sides and tube of a 10-inch pan, lining the bottom of the pan with waxed paper. Cream the shortening with sugar until fluffy. Add the poppyseed filling, mixing well. Add the chocolate, orange rind, and the jam. Add the egg yolks, 1 at a time, beating after each. Finally add the vanilla, mixing well. Sift the flour with the remaining dry ingredients. Add alternately with the sour cream, beginning and ending with the flour mixture. Beat the egg whites until stiff, using a clean bowl and beaters. Fold the stiffly beaten whites into the batter. Bake in a 350° oven for 1 hour 20 minutes. Cool the torte in the pan for 15 minutes on a rack. Remove from the pan, and cool the cake on a rack. Serve sprinkled with confectioners' sugar.

POPPYSEED BARS

1/2 cup + 2 tablespoons butter
1/2 cup sugar
3/4 teaspoon vanilla
3/4 cup grated almonds
1 1/2 cups sifted flour
2 ounces grated sweet chocolate
1/4 teaspoon cinnamon
1/8 teaspoon ginger
1/8 teaspoon mace
1 egg yolk
1 teaspoon egg white
1/4 cup poppyseed

Cream the butter and sugar together until light and fluffy; add the vanilla and almonds. Add the flour, chocolate, and spices, mixing well. Turn the dough into a greased 9-inch-square baking pan. Place in the refrigerator for 30 minutes. Beat together the egg yolk and egg white; brush on the surface of the pastry. Sprinkle the poppyseeds over the top of the dough. Bake in a 375° oven for 25 minutes. Cut into bars while warm. Yields 4 dozen.

MANDELBRODT

1 cup sugar
3 large eggs
6 tablespoons corn oil
Grated rind of 1 lemon
1 teaspoon lemon juice
1/4 teaspoon almond extract
2 3/4 cups flour
4 teaspoons baking powder
1/4 teaspoon salt
1/2 cup coarsely chopped almonds

Beat the sugar and eggs together until light and fluffy. Stir in the oil, lemon rind, lemon juice, and almond extract. Sift the flour, measure, and sift again with the baking powder and salt. Combine the dry ingredients with the egg mixture, adding the nuts. Mix together until it forms a ball of dough. Knead on a lightly floured board. Form into rolls 1-inch thick and 3-inches wide when flattened. Bake on a greased cooky sheet in a 350° oven for 40 to 45 minutes until light brown. Remove the rolls to a cutting board. Slice diagonally 1/2 inch thick, placing them cut side up on the baking sheet. Bake on the top shelf of the oven until brown on both sides. Yield: 3 dozen slices.

PASSOVER SPONGE CAKE

12 large eggs, separated
2 cups sugar
Juice and grated rind of 1 lemon
1/4 cup cold water
1 cup matzo meal cake flour
Pinch salt
1 cup potato flour

Beat the egg yolks with the sugar in an electric mixer until thick, creamy, and lighter in color. Add the lemon juice, rind, and cold water, stirring well. Mix the flours together. Stir them into the egg mixture a little at a time until the batter becomes thick. Beat the egg whites with a pinch of salt until they hold stiff peaks. Lightly fold the beaten whites into the yolks with a whisk. Line a 13x9x2-inch baking pan with waxed paper. Turn the batter into the pan. Bake in a 325° oven for 50 minutes to 1 hour until done. When the cake edges crisp, standing away from the pan, it is done. Invert, remove the paper, and cool. Serve cut in squares. Delicious with fruit.

HE SINAI PENINSULA
FOREMOST TOURIST ATTRACTION

STRUDEL

What is usually called strudel in delicatessens and even in some restaurants is definitely not the real thing. Strudel dough is really a tissue-thin leaf. When baked and ready to serve, it is crisp and incredibly flaky. Anything else is a rank imitation. Since I am Hungarian, I found that only in authentic Hungarian restaurants has the strudel compared with my memories of home.

You must see strudel dough being stretched to really get the hang of it. I recommend you use the strudel leaves sold in specialty food stores. Where these are not available use filo (phyllo) leaves, but they are not as good.

METHOD

Melt butter or fat. Spread out the leaves, each on a clean linen towel, (no more than 4 at a time). Drizzle fat over them with a spoon. Place the filling on 2/3 of the leaf, leaving a 1 1/2 inch margin on the side nearest to you and the 1/3 portion that is unfilled on the far side. Use the cloth to help get the roll started, rolling away from you. Rest the strudel, seam side down, on a teflon cooky sheet with sides. Brush the strudel with melted butter or fat. Bake in a 400° oven for 35 minutes until brown and crisp. Cut immediately into slices 2 inches thick. Sprinkle the strudel with confectioners' sugar if it has a sweet filling. Eat while fresh.

Since strudel leaves are quite expensive, they come in small quantities. The fillings listed on the following pages will fill 1 large strudel (homemade stretch dough) or 4 small leaves.

continued

Apple Filling: 1/2 cup sweet butter
3/4 cup bread crumbs
9 medium green apples or
9 cups thinly sliced apples
1/3 cup white raisins
1/2 cup sugar
2 teaspoons cinnamon
1/3 cup grated almonds

Spread 2/3 of the strudel dough with crumbs lightly sauteed in butter. Place a thin layer of 1/4 of the apples on the dough. The dough is very delicate. If you overload it with filling it will break when you roll it. Sprinkle with sugar mixed with cinnamon, raisins, and nuts.

Mohn Filling:

- 1/2 pound ground poppyseed
- 1/2 cup lekvar (plum puree)
- 1 cup scalded cream
- 1/4 cup white raisins
- 1/4 cup softened sweet butter
- 1/2 cup sugar
- Grated rind of 1 lemon
- 2 teaspoons cinnamon

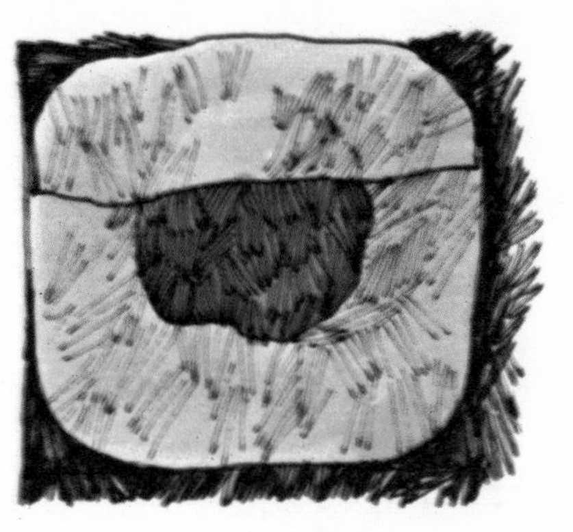

Heat the poppyseed with the lekvar and cream in a covered pot. The mixture should be stirred frequently until thick. Add the remaining ingredients; cool.

continued

Cabbage Filling: 1/2 large cored head cabbage
Pepper
Bread crumbs
Pinch salt
Sugar
Melted chicken fat

Grate the cabbage; sprinkle with salt. Squeeze out the moisture. Saute the cabbage in fat until it starts to brown. Arrange the cabbage on the strudel leaf, sprinkle with bread crumbs and season well with pepper and sugar. Baste the strudel with melted chicken fat.

Cherry Filling: 1 1/3 cups ground almonds
Bread crumbs
4 cups fresh pitted cherries
2/3 cup sugar
1 teaspoon cinnamon
1 teaspoon almond extract

Sprinkle the nuts evenly on the strudel leaves. Mix the cherries with the almond extract. Put a layer of cherries on the strudel leaves. Then add some bread crumbs, more if the cherries are fresh. Mix the cinnamon and sugar; sprinkle on the cherries.

Cheese Filling: See recipe on page 46.

ALL ABOUT BAGELS

Without bagels how would we eat lox? Bagels, to the uninitiated, are doughnut shaped rolls, but there the resemblance ends. Any doughnut with the consistency of a bagel would have to be a fossil! Bagels should be eaten the same day that they are made. It is possible to serve them one day old by splitting them crosswise and toasting them. But any left after that are only good as weapons for self-defense. Throw an old bagel at an enemy; but beware – it may be lethal.

Bagels come in many flavors – plain, onion, poppyseed, pumpernickel, and some bakeries even have some in a non-traditional oblong shape. Never cut a bagel vertically. The only way a bagel is good is with something spread on it or stuffed inside it. You must use a very sharp knife when halving a bagel. Since they are not very large, watch out for the fingers! Some bakeries sell bagel cutters which take all the challenges out of life!

Serve sweet butter, cream cheese, and plenty of lox with bagels for breakfast.

They are also good with brunch, lunch, and assorted snacks throughout the day. Bagels are not eaten with a meat meal because they are not really as good with nothing on them, and butter cannot traditionally be served with meat.

Try using bagels for sandwiches. Salami, bologna, pastrami, corned beef, and chopped liver are delicious with mustard on a bagel. Good cheeses are also delicious in a bagel which is spread with sweet butter. Fillings should be hearty. Never make a bagel sandwich with just 1 slice of meat, cheese, or lox. All Jewish sandwiches have fillings at least 1/2 inch thick.

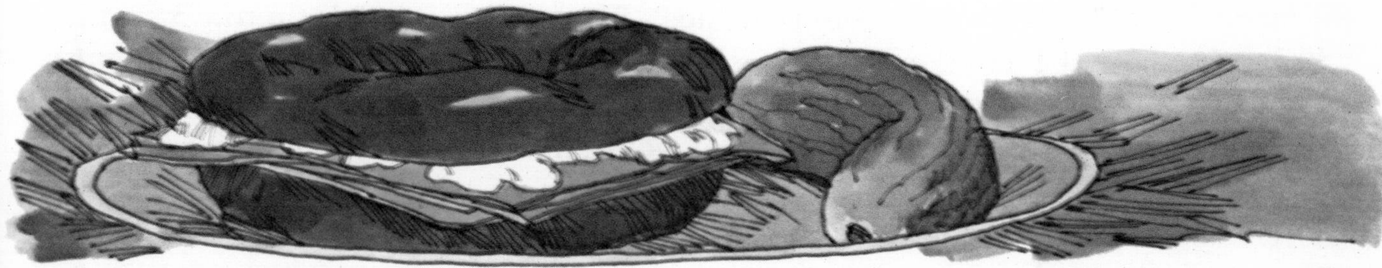

ALL ABOUT CHICKEN FAT

Chicken fat is one of the most important ingredients used in Jewish cooking. It is essential to achieve just the right 'tam' in preparing Jewish foods. You can buy rendered chicken fat in some poultry markets or Jewish delicatessens (Do not use imitations!). It is surprisingly easy to prepare, and can last for months at a time. Rendered chicken fat is light gold in color, and the consistency of homogenized shortening. Foods browned in it have a deeper color, a crisper texture, and a better flavor.

HOW TO RENDER CHICKEN FAT: Put 2 pounds of room-temperature chicken fat into a heavy skillet over medium-low heat. Turn the fat from time to time so it will all render. The fat is ready to use when the cracklings are hard, with no pockets of fat. (This process takes from 2 to 3 hours.) Remove the cracklings from the pan with a fork, and drain them well. These are a delicacy (some people call them Jewish popcorn and like to eat them out of hand), and can be used in chopped liver. When cool, transfer fat to a sterile jar, cover, and refrigerate.

HOW TO SHOP AT A KOSHER DELICATESSEN

All delicatessens carry a complete line of salami, bologna, corned beef, pastrami, pickled tongue, kishke, smoked fish, and so on. Where the owner or his wife make the foods you are in luck. Then you can enjoy homemade cole slaw, potato salad, cucumber salad, chopped herring, and chopped liver. Look for homemade sauerkraut,especially with apples. Do not overlook the pickle barrel. The best ones are still crisp, not too done.

The blintzes and knishes vary depending on the owner's ethnic background. Find out where the owner came from – Germany, Poland, Hungary, or Russia. Owners are notoriously voluble. Ask if they make any special foods on occasion. This is the way to sample the most interesting Jewish delights.

Buy Jewish breads and rolls to eat with this food. Question the delicatessen owners about how to prepare and serve anything strange to you. They are usually eager to share their knowledge with you.

MENUS

Here is a section of menus featuring entire gourmet Jewish meals for different days and family occasions.

Food plays a very important part in the Jewish family life because of the many historical traditions and religious laws governing the preparation and serving of food. If you are Jewish, you may learn something new from these menus to help you add variety to your family's mealtime pleasure. If you are not Jewish, you will find a whole new world of tasty, wholesome, stick-to-the-ribs menus. Too many gentiles go through life without ever knowing what Jewish food is like, and once they have found out, they will thank you for an introduction to a whole new world of dining.

These menus are suitable for your family meals or for entertaining. Enjoy!

SUNDAY BRUNCH

Juice or Fresh Fruit Cup
Blintzes with Sour Cream and Jam
Smoked Whitefish
Pickled Herring
Bagels and Rye Bread
Hard-Boiled Eggs
Sweet Butter
Coffee

ISRAELI BREAKFAST

Juices
Shredded Carrots in Orange Juice
Cold Hard-Boiled Eggs
Farmer Cheese
Tomato Wedges
Mixed Salad with Lemon and Oil Dressing
Herring
Sardines
Kuchen with Chocolate Poppyseed Filling
Coffee - Tea

ROSH HASHANAH DINNER

Fresh Fruit Cup
Chicken Soup with Mandlen
Roast Turkey
Stuffed Helzel
Haimische Vegetable Tzimmes
Potato Kugel
Cucumber Salad
Cranberry Sauce
Challah
Honey Cake
Poppyseed Bars
Dates
Nuts
Tea

ISRAELI DINNER

Matbeylah
Humus
Pita
Bean and Barley Soup
Moroccan-Style Lamb
Kasha with Varnishkes
Sponge Cake
Fresh Fruit
Tea or Turkish Coffee

SHABBAT DINNER

Chopped Liver
Chicken Soup with Noodles
Roast Chicken
Stuffed Helzel
Potato Kugel
Carrots
Challah
Sponge Cake
Fruit
Tea

SHABBAT DINNER

Gefilte Fish
Red and White Horseradish
Tomato Soup with Rice
Chicken Fricassee
Tzibbele Potatoes
Sweet-and-Sour Green Beans
Cooked Carrots
Challah
Honey Cake
Fruit
Coffee - Tea

SHAVUOT SUPPER

Pareve Chopped Liver
Cold Beet Borscht
Blintzes with Traditional Cheese Filling
South Cream with Jams
Coffeecake
Coffee

SHAVUOT SUPPER

Challah
Cold Cabbage Borscht
Baked Shad
The Kugel with Tam
Cucumber Salad
Cheesecake to Serve the Mishpocheh
Coffee - Tea

SUPPER

Knishes
Stuffed Breast of Veal
Sweet and Sour Red Cabbage
Farfel
Poppyseed Torte
Coffee - Tea

SUPPER

Chopped Herring
Split-Pea Soup
Beef Gulyas
Galuska
Cooked Cauliflower
Cucumber Salad
Cherry Strudel
Coffee - Tea

SUPPER

Yenta's Lentil Soup
Meat Loaf with Tomato Sauce
Kasha and Varnishkes
Cooked Asparagus
Mandelbrodt
Fruit
Coffee - Tea

SUPPER

Essig Fleisch
Noodles
Cucumber Salad
Rye Bread
Honey Cake
Coffee - Tea

INDEX